AAT

Qualifications and Credit Framework (QCF)

LEVEL 4 DIPLOMA IN ACCOUNTING

TEXT

External Auditing

2011 Edition

First edition July 2010

Second edition June 2011

ISBN 9780 7517 9741 1 (Previous edition 9780 7517 8572 2)

British Library Cataloguing-in-Publication Data
A catalogue record for this book is available from the British
Library

Published by

BPP Learning Media Ltd
BPP House
Aldine Place
London
W12 8AA

www.bpp.com/learningmedia

Printed in the United Kingdom

CONTENTS

A NOTE ABOUT COPYRIGHT

INTRODUCTION

Since July 2010 the AAT's assessments have fallen within the **Qualifications and Credit Framework** and most papers are now assessed by way of an on demand **computer based assessment**. BPP Learning Media has invested heavily to produce new ground breaking market leading resources. In particular, our **suite of online resources** ensures that you are prepared for online testing by means of an online environment where tasks mimic the style of the AAT's assessment tasks.

The BPP range of resources comprises:

- **Texts**, covering all the knowledge and understanding needed by students, with numerous illustrations of 'how it works', practical examples and tasks for you to use to consolidate your learning. The majority of tasks within the texts have been written in an interactive style that reflects the style of the online tasks the AAT will set. Texts are available in our traditional paper format and, in addition, as ebooks which can be downloaded to your PC or laptop.

- **Question Banks**, including additional learning questions plus the AAT's practice assessment and a number of other full practice assessments. Full answers to all questions and assessments, prepared by BPP Learning Media Ltd, are included. Our question banks are provided free of charge in an online environment which mimics the AAT's testing environment. This enables you to familiarise yourself with the environment in which you will be tested.

- **Passcards**, which are handy pocket-sized revision tools designed to fit in a handbag or briefcase to enable you to revise anywhere at anytime. All major points are covered in the Passcards which have been designed to assist you in consolidating knowledge.

- **Workbooks**, which have been designed to cover the units that are assessed by way of project/case study. The workbooks contain many practical tasks to assist in the learning process and also a sample assessment or project to work through.

- **Lecturers' resources**, providing a further bank of tasks, answers and full practice assessments for classroom use, available separately only to lecturers whose colleges adopt BPP Learning Media material. The practice assessments within the lecturers' resources are available in both paper format and online in e format. What fantastic news: you can now give your students an online mock.

This Text for External Auditing has been written specifically to ensure comprehensive yet concise coverage of the AAT's new learning outcomes and assessment criteria. It is fully up to date as at June 2011 and reflects both the AAT's unit guide and the practice assessment provided by the AAT.

Each chapter contains:

- clear, step by step explanation of the topic

- logical progression and linking from one chapter to the next

- numerous illustrations of 'how it works'

- interactive tasks within the text of the chapter itself, with answers at the back of the book. In general, these tasks have been written in the interactive form that students will see in their real assessments

- test your learning questions of varying complexity, again with answers supplied at the back of the book. In general, these test questions have been written in the interactive form that students will see in their real assessments

The emphasis in all tasks and test questions is on the practical application of the skills acquired.

If you have any comments about this book, please e-mail suedexter@bpp.com or write to Sue Dexter, Publishing Director, BPP Learning Media Ltd, BPP House, Aldine Place, London W12 8AA.

ASSESSMENT STRATEGY

The Assessment consists of two sections of 15 tasks each, including tasks requiring extended written responses from the learner.

Section 1 will focus on testing learners' knowledge and understanding of the key concepts of external auditing. Section 2 will assess learners' skills in applying knowledge of auditing financial statements.

Learners will normally be assessed by computer-based assessment (CBA), which will include extended writing tasks, and will be required to demonstrate competence in both sections of the assessment.

Competency

For the purpose of assessment the competency level for AAT assessment is set at 70 per cent. The level descriptor below describes the ability and skills students at this level must successfully demonstrate to achieve competence.

QCF Level descriptor	**Summary**
	Achievement at level 4 reflects the ability to identify and use relevant understanding, methods and skills to address problems that are well defined but complex and non-routine. It includes taking responsibility for overall courses of action as well as exercising autonomy and judgement within fairly broad parameters. It also reflects understanding of different perspectives or approaches within an area of study or work.
	Knowledge and understanding
	<ul><li>Practical, theoretical or technical understanding to address problems that are well defined but complex and non routine</li><li>Analyse, interpret and evaluate relevant information and ideas</li><li>Be aware of the nature and approximate scope of the area of study or work</li><li>Have an informed awareness of different perspectives or approaches within the area of study or work</li></ul>
	Application and action
	<ul><li>Address problems that are complex and non routine, while normally fairly well defined</li><li>Identify, adapt and use appropriate methods and skills</li><li>Initiate and use appropriate investigation to inform actions</li><li>Review the effectiveness and appropriateness of methods, actions and results</li></ul>
	Autonomy and accountability
	<ul><li>Take responsibility for courses of action, including, where relevant, responsibility for the work of others</li><li>Exercise autonomy and judgement within broad but generally well-defined parameters</li></ul>

AAT UNIT GUIDE

External audit

Introduction

Please read this document in conjunction with the standards for the unit.

The purpose of the unit

- To ensure that learners understand the essence and objectives of the audit process and the implications of the regulatory requirements and pronouncements of the professional bodies.

- To enable learners to contribute to the conduct of all stages of an audit, including planning, gathering evidence, concluding and reporting findings, in accordance with International Standards on Auditing.

Learning Objectives

In the Principles of External Auditing unit learners develop an understanding of the legal and regulatory requirements relating to external audit engagements and how the external audit process meets those requirements. Learners should demonstrate a knowledge of internal controls within accounting systems and the different types of audit evidence. Learners should understand the role of materiality and risk assessment in the external audit process.

In the Auditing Financial Statements unit learners should be able to contribute to the audit process by assessing the risk of misstatement in the financial statements and by selecting sufficient and appropriate methods of obtaining audit evidence in order to address the risks identified. Learners should be able to document an organisation's internal control system, identify deficiencies, understand the implications of deficiencies and make recommendations for improvement. Learners should be able to draw conclusions which are consistent with the results of their work and recommend the nature of an audit opinion to be given in an audit report.

Learning outcomes

Principles of External Audit (Knowledge)

- Demonstrate an understanding of the legal and professional standards required for an external auditor

- Understand the organisation's external auditing procedures

- Understand a range of auditing techniques and know which to use when planning audits on different aspects of the system

- Understand a range of audit documentation and recognise the appropriateness

Auditing Financial Statements (Skills)

- Be able to help plan an audit accurately identifying areas to be verified and any associated risks

- Undertake an audit under supervision

- Prepare draft reports for approval

QCF Unit	Learning Outcome	Assessment Criteria	Covered in Chapter
Principles of External Audit (Knowledge)	Demonstrate an understanding of the legal and professional standards required for an external auditor	Explain the legal and ethical duties of auditors, including the content of reports and the definition of proper records	1
		Explain the liability of auditors under contract and negligence including liability to third parties	2
		Explain the relevant legislation and auditing standards	1/2
		Define audit risk and how it applies to external audit	5
		Define materiality and explain its application to auditing	5
	Understand the organisation's external auditing procedures	Describe the organisations systems and external auditing procedures	3
		Describe the features of accounting systems including purchases, sales, inventory, expenses, statement of financial position (balance sheet) items and payroll	3
		Identify principles of control and when they should be used including separation of functions, the need for authorisation, recording, custody vouching and verification	3

QCF Unit	Learning Outcome	Assessment Criteria	Covered in Chapter
	Understand a range of auditing techniques and know which to use when planning audits on different aspects of the system	Describe the different verification techniques that can be used and explain what type of item could be audited by this method. Methods to include physical examination, reperformance, third party confirmation, vouching, documentary evidence and identification of unusual items	4/6
		Identify different sampling techniques used in auditing and describe where these could be used including confidence levels, selection techniques including random numbers, interval sampling and stratified sampling	6
		Explain tests of control and substantive procedures and their links to the audit objective	4/6
		Explain the auditing techniques that should be used in an IT environment	4
		Explain how management feedback, that includes systems weaknesses, clerical/accounting mistakes, disagreement regarding accounting policies or treatment, can be used when planning an audit	3/6
	Understand a range of audit documentation and recognise the appropriateness	Explain the features of recording and evaluating systems including the use of conventional symbols, flowcharts, internal control questionnaires (ICQs) and checklists	4
		Recognise the importance of audit files and working papers and their role in the audit process	1

QCF Unit	Learning Outcome	Assessment Criteria	Covered in Chapter
Auditing Financial Statements (Skills)	Be able to help plan an audit accurately identifying areas to be verified and any associated risks	Identify the accounting systems under review and accurately record them on appropriate working papers	3/4/5/6
		Correctly identify the control framework	
		Accurately assess risks associated with the accounting system and its controls	
		Correctly record significant weaknesses in internal control	
		Identify account balances to be verified and the associated risks	
		Select an appropriate sample for testing	
		Select or devise appropriate tests in accordance with auditing principles and agree them with the audit supervisor	
		Provide clear information and recommendations for the proposed audit plan and submit it to the appropriate person for consideration	
	Undertake an audit under supervision	Conduct tests correctly, properly record tests results and draw valid conclusions from them as specified in the audit plan	
		Establish the existence, completeness, ownership, valuation and description of assets and liabilities and gather appropriate evidence to support these findings	
		Identify all matters of an unusual nature and refer them promptly to the audit supervisor	

QCF Unit	Learning Outcome	Assessment Criteria	Covered in Chapter
		Identify and record material and significant errors, deficiencies or other variations from standard and report them to the audit supervisor	
	Prepare draft reports for approval	Prepare and submit clear and concise draft reports illustrating constructive and practicable recommendations in line with organisational procedures Agree preliminary conclusions and recommendations with the audit supervisor Follow confidentiality and security procedures at all times.	2/4/10

Delivery guidance

1. **Demonstrate an understanding of the legal and professional standards required for an external auditor**

1.1 Explain the legal and ethical duties of auditors, including the content of reports and the definition of proper records

- Describe the:
  - Legal requirements such as the UK Companies Act 2006 requirement for auditors to express an opinion on whether the financial statements give a true and fair view
  - Objective of an audit of financial statements as set out in paragraphs 3 to 12 of ISA 200 *Overall Objectives of the Independent Auditor and the Conduct of an Audit in Accordance with International Standards on Auditing* and in paragraphs 5 to 8 of ISA 240 *The Auditor's Responsibilities Relating to Fraud in an Audit of Financial Statements*.
  - Respective responsibilities of management and external auditors in relation to the financial statements.
  - Role of independence and objectivity

- Describe the elements of an audit report as required by paragraphs 12 to 18 and 21 to 24 of ISA 700 *Forming an Opinion and Reporting on Financial Statements*.

- Describe the nature of adequate accounting records such as those required by Section 386 of the UK Companies Act 2006.

1.2 <u>Explain the liability of auditors under contract and negligence including liability to third parties:</u>

Describe the:

- Sources of liability including:

    - Liability to the company and shareholders under contract; and

    - Liability to third parties under tort of negligence when there is a duty of care

- Consequences of audit failures including damages and legal and professional penalties.

- Manner in which auditors may reduce the risk of exposure to claims for damages including;

    - Limited liability agreements between auditor and client including proportionate liability and liability caps;

    - Limited liability partnerships;

    - Professional indemnity insurance; and

    - Use of disclaimers (e.g. Bannerman paragraph).

1.3 <u>Explain the relevant legislation and auditing standards</u>

Describe the standard setting process, in particular the:

- Roles of the IAASB and, in the UK the APB, in promoting high standards of auditing, meeting the developing needs of users of financial information and ensuring public confidence in the audit process.

- Role of International Standards on Auditing in promoting audit quality and advancing global convergence.

1.4 <u>Define audit risk and how it applies to external audit</u>

- Describe the components of the audit risk model i.e. inherent risk, control risk and detection risk.

- Explain the relationship between the components, in particular, how auditors manage detection risk in order to keep audit risk at an acceptably low level.

- Explain how factors such as the entity's operating environment and its system of internal control affect the risk of misstatement.

1.5 Define materiality and explain its application to auditing

- Describe the methods used to calculate a materiality threshold for planning an audit including materiality for the financial statements as a whole and performance materiality as required by paragraphs 10 to14 of ISA 320 *Materiality in Planning and Performing an Audit*.

- Explain the role of materiality in planning an audit and evaluating misstatements.

2. Understanding the organisation's external procedures

2.1 Describe the organisation's systems and external auditing procedures

- Describe the accounting systems relevant to the audit of the financial statements.

- Explain why auditors need to obtain an understanding of internal control activities relevant to the financial information and how weaknesses in the systems limit the extent of auditors' reliance on those systems.

2.2 Describe the features of accounting systems including purchases, sales, inventory, expenses, statement of financial position (balance sheet) items and payroll

For each of the major accounting systems (purchases, revenue, payroll, inventory, non-current assets, bank and cash), describe the:

- Control objectives;
- Risks/exposure if control objectives not met; and
- Procedures required to meet the control objectives.

2.3 Identify principles of control and when they should be used including separation of functions, the need for authorisation, recording, custody vouching and verification

- Define internal control and its components as set out in paragraph 4c of ISA 315 *Identifying and Assessing the Risks of Material Misstatement Through Understanding the Entity and its Environment* including:

  - Control environment

  - Control activities, including performance reviews, information processing, physical controls and segregation of duties

  - Monitoring of controls

- Describe the limitations of internal controls.

3. Understand a range of auditing techniques and know which to use when planning audits on different aspects of the system

3.1 Describe the different verification techniques that can be used and explain what type of item could be audited by this method. Methods to include physical examination, reperformance, third party confirmation, vouching, documentary evidence and identification of unusual items

- Describe the procedures for obtaining sufficient appropriate audit evidence as set out in paragraphs A10 to A25 of ISA 500 *Audit Evidence* and the limitations of each source of evidence.

- Describe the assertions regarding, the recognition, measurement, presentation and disclosures of the various elements of financial statements as set out in paragraph A111 of ISA 315 *Identifying and Assessing the risk of Material Misstatement through Understanding the Entity and its Environment.*

- Explain the impact of the assertions on the direction of testing e.g. tracing source documents to ledger accounts when checking for understatement and vouching entries in the ledger accounts to source documents when testing for overstatement.

3.2 Identify different sampling techniques used in auditing and describe where these could be used including confidence levels, selection techniques including random numbers, interval sampling and stratified sampling

- Define audit sampling, including statistical and non-statistical sampling.

- Explain why it may be more appropriate to use 100% examination or a selection of specific items.

- Describe the characteristics of the different methods used in selecting items for checking.

- Describe the factors that affect sample sizes as set out in appendix 2 of ISA 530 *Audit Sampling*.

3.3 Explain tests of control and substantive procedures and their links to the audit objective

- Define tests of control and substantive procedures.

- Describe how auditors use tests of control when planning to rely on internal controls relevant to financial information.

- Explain why it is appropriate to use a mixture of tests of control and substantive procedures or substantive procedures only.

- Describe the methods used to test controls.

- Describe how tests of details and analytical procedures are used in the context of financial statement assertions.

3.4 Explain the auditing techniques that should be used in an IT environment

- Describe computer-assisted audit techniques (CAATs) such as test data and audit software.

- Explain how CAATs test controls and check the reliability of balances.

3.5 Explain how management feedback, that includes systems weaknesses, clerical/accounting mistakes, disagreement regarding accounting policies or treatment, can be used when planning an audit

- Explain how the attitude and integrity of management impacts on the:

  - Control environment

  - Risk of misstatement in the financial statements through fraud

  - Need for auditors to exercise professional scepticism.

4. Understand a range of audit documentation and recognise the appropriateness

4.1 Explain the features of recording and evaluating systems including the use of conventional symbols, flowcharts, internal; control questionnaires (ICQs) and checklists

- Describe the features of flowcharts, ICQs and checklists.

- Explain the role of systems records in determining the audit strategy.

- Describe the merits and limitations of using standardised questionnaires and checklists.

4.2 Recognise the importance of audit files and working papers and their role in the audit process

- Explain the role of audit documentation in providing evidence as a basis for the auditor's report and the need to retain working papers for future reference.

- Describe the form and content of working papers as required by paragraphs 2 to 11 of ISA 230 *Audit Documentation*.

Auditing Financial Statements (Skills)

Learning Outcomes	Assessment Criteria	Guidance for delivery
1. **Be able to help plan an audit accurately identifying areas to be verified and any associated risks**	1.1 Identify the accounting systems under review and accurately record them on appropriate working papers 1.2 Correctly identify the control framework 1.3 Accurately assess risks associated with the accounting system and its controls 1.4 Correctly record significant weaknesses in internal control 1.5 Identify account balances to be verified and the associated risks 1.6 Select an appropriate sample for testing 1.7 Select or devise appropriate tests in accordance with auditing principles and agree them with the audit supervisor 1.8 Provide clear information and recommendations for the proposed audit plan and submit it to the appropriate person for consideration	From background information, including financial information, provided about an entity: – Identify the key accounting systems to be audited – Identify features of the organisation's corporate culture which contribute to the strengthening or weakening of the control environment – Complete ICQs relating to the accounting systems – Design tests of control to check the effectiveness of the controls on which the auditor plans to rely – Identify deficiencies in internal control which must be communicated to those charged with governance – Identify factors relating to the entity's operating environment and system of internal control which give rise to risk of material misstatement in the financial statements – Calculate a materiality threshold by applying given percentages to key figures in the financial statements – Apply analytical procedures to financial information to identify movements out of line with expectation and possible risk of misstatement Design audit procedures to address the risk of misstatements identified at the planning stage.

Learning Outcomes	Assessment Criteria	Guidance for delivery
2. **Undertake an audit under supervision**	2.1 Conduct tests correctly, properly record tests results and draw valid conclusions from them and specified in the audit plan 2.2 Establish the existence, completeness, ownership, valuation and description of assets and liabilities and gather appropriate evidence to support these findings 2.3 Identify all matters of an unusual natures and refer them promptly to the audit supervisor 2.4 Identify and record material and significant errors, deficiencies or other variations from standard and report them to the audit supervisor	Design procedures relating to the relevant assertions for key figures in the financial statements, in particular: – Non-current assets; – Inventory; – Receivables; – Cash and bank; – Borrowings; – Payables; – Provisions; – Revenue; – Payroll and other expenses. Draw conclusions based on the materiality of individual misstatements or aggregation of individually immaterial misstatements or the nature of misstatements as required by paragraphs 5 to 15 of ISA 450 *Evaluation of Misstatements Identified During the Audit.*
3. **Prepare draft reports for approval**	3.1 Prepare and submit clear and concise draft reports illustrating constructive and practicable recommendations in line with organisational procedures	Identify, from a description of a client's accounting system, deficiencies in internal control that should be communicated to management in the form of a description of the deficiencies and an explanation of their potential effect and recommendations for improvement as required by paragraphs 7 to 11 of ISA 265 *Communicating Deficiencies in Internal Control to those*

Learning Outcomes	Assessment Criteria	Guidance for delivery

	3.2 Agree preliminary conclusions and recommendations with the audit supervisor
	
	3.3 Follow confidentiality and security procedures at all times
		Charged with Governance and Management
		
		For a given scenario:
		
		– Draw conclusions, as required by paragraphs 6 to 10 of ISA 705 *Modifications to the Opinion in the Independent Auditor's Report*, on the effect on the audit of:
		  – Uncorrected material misstatements; and
		  – Inability to obtain sufficient audit evidence to conclude that the
		  – Financial statements are free from material misstatement.
		
		Determine whether to provide a qualified, adverse or disclaimer of opinion.
		
		– Determine as required by paragraphs 6 to 7 ISA 706 *Emphasis of Matter Paragraphs and Other Matter Paragraphs in the Independent Auditor's Report*, when to draw users of financial statements' attention to matters appropriately presented or disclosed in the financial statements (Emphasis of Matter Paragraph)
		
		Recognise situations when the professional duty of confidentiality is overridden by a legal or public duty as in the case of suspected money laundering and take the required course of action.

International and UK Terminology Comparison

UK law requires certain matters relating to audit, and UK law uses UK terminology in respect of accounting matters. This Text and your studies are based on International terminology. In this book, you will find UK terminology where UK legal issues are referred to (mainly in Chapter 1) and thereafter, international terminology will be used.

This section sets out a comparison of the terminology used:

International	UK
Statement of Financial Position	Balance Sheet
Statement of comprehensive income	Profit and loss account (P&L)
Retained earnings	Profit and loss reserve
Non-current assets	Fixed assets
Property, plant & equipment	Tangible fixed assets
Inventories	Stock
Trade receivables	Trade debtors
Current liabilities	Creditors: Amounts falling due within one year
Non-current liabilities	Creditors: Amounts falling due after more than one year
Trade payables	Trade creditors
Deferred tax liability	Deferred tax provision
Sales tax	Value Added Tax (VAT)

chapter 1:
THE BUSINESS ENVIRONMENT

chapter coverage 📖

In this chapter we outline the basic legal requirements relating to a company, including the requirement to have an audit, the main subject of our Text. The topics covered are:

✍ Requirement to keep accounting records

✍ Requirement to have an audit

✍ Introduction to the audit firm

REQUIREMENT TO KEEP ACCOUNTING RECORDS

Implications of registering a company

A COMPANY is an entity registered as such under the Companies Act 2006. The entity must meet certain requirements in order to be registered as a company.

Registration of a company gives the owners (usually known as shareholders) benefits such as limited liability for any debts the company incur, as the company is treated as being separate from the owners themselves. This means that shareholders will only ever be liable for the cost of their shares. Creditors of the company cannot sue the shareholders as individuals for any company debts. Another benefit is that the owners of a company do not have to manage the business of the company themselves, as they can employ separate managers or directors, although they can be managers and directors themselves if they so wish.

However, registration also imposes a number of legal requirements on the company and its owners and managers, many of which are found in the Companies Act under which the company is registered.

Task 1

Set out the major implications of registering a business as a company.

Accounting records

One of the requirements is to keep accounting records. ACCOUNTING RECORDS are records of the financial dealings of the company. What actually constitutes suitable financial records is defined by the Companies Act 2006, which states:

'Every company must keep adequate accounting records. Adequate accounting records means records that are sufficient to:

(a) Show and explain the company's transactions,

(b) Disclose with reasonable accuracy, at any time, the financial position of the company at that time, and

(c) Enable the directors to ensure that any accounts required to be prepared comply with the requirements of this Act.'

In other words, the accounting records must be kept in sufficient detail that someone qualified to do so, say an accountant, could construct a balance sheet (statement of financial position) or profit and loss account (statement of comprehensive income) from them at any time. You should be familiar with both of these statements from your other AAT studies.

One thing that you should note is that the requirement to keep accounting records is a duty of the **directors** (managers), not the **shareholders** (owners).

The requirement to have an audit, which we shall move on to soon, is based on the fact that in a company, the owners and managers do not necessarily have to be the same people.

Requirements for all companies

The Act gives more detail about what accounting records should contain:

- **Money received and spent** by the company from day-to-day
- What the money is related to (eg, **sales, purchases and wages**)
- Details of the **assets and liabilities** of the company

You should be familiar with all these terms from your previous AAT studies.

Requirements for companies dealing in goods

The Act goes on to say that if the company has stock (also known as inventory) it should keep details of stock as well as:

- Statements of stock held at the financial year-end

- Records of the stock count from which the above statement is prepared

- Statements of goods sold and purchased to enable the goods and buyers or sellers to be identified (that is, invoices)

Location of accounting records

Accounting records must be kept at the registered office of the company (which is a location specified as part of the company registration procedures), or at another place which the directors think is fit.

The records must be available so that the company's officers (for example, the auditors) can inspect them.

Time period for holding accounting records

The length of time a company must keep the records for depends on what type of company has been registered.

If a private limited (Limited or Ltd) company has been registered, then the directors have to keep the financial records for three years from the date on which they were made.

If a public limited (plc) company has been registered, then the directors have to keep the financial records for six years from the date on which they were made.

In practice, most companies keep their records for at least six years to meet requirements of other laws, for example, tax law, which requires that records must be available for longer.

Task 2

Complete the statement below on adequate accounting records by filling in the gaps with terms from the following selection.

- Reasonable accuracy
- Total accuracy
- At the year-end
- At all times
- Market value
- Financial position

Adequate accounting records are records sufficient to disclose with
...., the ....
.... of the company, ...

Failure to comply with the requirements

If the directors do not maintain suitable accounting records, they are guilty of a criminal offence subject to imprisonment and/or a fine.

Task 3

Set out what accounting records the directors of a company need to maintain.

Task 4

Imagine it is December 20X5.

Lilac Ltd has a file of invoices dated January 20X3 – April 20X3. Purple plc has a file of invoices which only contains invoices from January 20X3.

State whether the following statements are True or False in respect of invoice retention.

	Options
Lilac Ltd may dispose of its file in January 20X6.	True
	False
Purple plc may dispose of these files of invoices in February 20X9.	True
	False

REQUIREMENT TO HAVE AN AUDIT

An AUDIT is an examination by a qualified independent examiner to enhance the confidence of intended users in the financial statements. The independent examiner (auditor) expresses an opinion that the financial statements have been prepared in accordance with an applicable financial reporting framework.

The FINANCIAL STATEMENTS of a company are the balance sheet, profit and loss account and the related notes. They may also include a cash flow statement and a statement of total recognised gains and losses and the directors' report if required by the law and accounting standards.

Financial statements are created by the directors of a company for the benefit of the owners, so that the owners can see whether their investment is doing as well as they would like. The financial statements should be prepared in accordance with the law and accounting standards.

We look in more detail at the definition of an audit in the next chapter.

A registered company is required by the Companies Act 2006 to be subject to an audit of its financial statements.

A few companies are allowed not to have an audit if they meet certain requirements.

Exemptions from the audit requirement

Small companies

Companies are permitted not to have an audit if they qualify as small companies:

- Turnover (reported sales) for the year is less than £6,500,000
- Balance sheet total for the year is less than £3,260,000
- A private (Ltd) company
- Not a bank or insurance company
- Not part of an ineligible group of companies
- Qualifies as a small company for accounting purposes

A small company that is a charity must meet different requirements to be exempt from audit.

Dormant companies

A DORMANT COMPANY is a company which has had no accounting transactions required to be recorded by the Companies Act during the relevant period.

A dormant company is permitted not to have an audit if it:

- Has been dormant since it was registered as a company
- Has been dormant since the end of the previous financial year

and:

- Is a small company (or would be if it were not a plc)
- Is not required to produce group accounts
- Is not a bank or insurance company

Task 5

Lemon Ltd has a turnover of £4,000,000 and a balance sheet total of £2 million.

Pear plc has a turnover of £600,000 and a balance sheet total of £1 million.

Lime Ltd has a turnover of £7 million and a balance sheet total of £2.6 million.

Lychee Ltd has a turnover of £200,000 and a balance sheet total of £750,000. It is part of the Fruit group of companies.

Peach plc has not had any transactions that needed to be recorded in the year.

State which one of the following options correctly shows which companies are required to have an audit.

Pear and Peach ☐

Pear, Lime and Peach ☐

Pear, Lime and Lychee ☐

Pear, Lime, Lychee and Lemon ☐

INTRODUCTION TO THE AUDIT FIRM

In the rest of this Text you will learn about the practical aspects of carrying out an audit. You should assume that you are a new audit trainee in a firm of accountants.

The narrator of the rest of the book will be your mentor at the firm, who will explain the basics of auditing to you. He will show you 'how it works' by using examples of auditing clients of the firm. Remember, auditing is a practical subject. You must be able to think of yourself as an auditor, even if you do not practice auditing techniques in your everyday job.

CHAPTER OVERVIEW

- Companies are required to maintain accounting records

- Accounting records comprise records of cash received and spent (and in respect of what), assets, liabilities, and where required, stock records

- Private (Ltd) companies are required to keep records for three years, and public (plc) companies for six years

- Companies are required to have an audit of financial statements

- Some companies are exempt from the audit requirement, if they are small or dormant businesses

Keywords

A **company** – is an entity registered as such under the Companies Act 2006

Accounting records – are records of the financial activities of the company

An **audit** – is an examination by a qualified independent examiner to enhance the confidence of intended users in the financial statements

The **financial statements** of a company are the balance sheet, profit and loss account and the related notes. They may also include a cash flow statement and a statement of total recognised gains and losses if required

A **dormant company** – is a company which has had no accounting transactions required to be recorded by the Companies Act during the relevant period

TEST YOUR LEARNING

Test 1 Complete the following statement by filling in the gaps using the items in the pick list below.

A .... is an .... registered as such under the Companies Act 2006.

Pick list

Company

Entity

Test 2 Which one of the following statements is not an implication of registering a company?

It is seen as distinct from its owners ☐

It is required to have an audit, unless exempt ☐

It must keep accounting records ☐

It must be managed by its owners ☐

Test 3 State whether the following are True or False in respect of a company's accounting records.

	Options
Companies must keep records that disclose with reasonable accuracy the company's position at any time.	True False
All companies must keep records of inventory.	True False
All companies should keep accounting records for at least six years.	True False

Test 4 All companies are required to have an audit of financial statements unless they are exempt. Select whether the following companies are exempt and why.

	Options
Puma Limited, a company with a turnover of £7,000,000 and balance sheet total of £3,000,000.	Not exempt Exempt – small Exempt – dormant
Jaguar plc, a company that has not recorded a transaction for two years.	Not exempt Exempt – small Exempt – dormant
Cheetah Ltd, a subsidiary of Fast Cats plc. Cheetah's turnover is £3,000 and its balance sheet total is £200,000.	Not exempt Exempt – small Exempt – dormant
Lion plc, a company with a turnover of £5,000,000 and balance sheet total of £2,100,000.	Not exempt Exempt – small Exempt – dormant

Test 5 Leopard Limited is a trading company which manufactures fabrics. It has a turnover of £900,000 and a balance sheet total of £4 million.

Task

Set out the Companies Act requirements covered in this chapter in relation to Leopard Limited.

chapter 2:
INTRODUCTION TO AUDIT

chapter coverage 📖

Before you implement any practical audit techniques, you need to understand what an audit is, and some of the legal requirements in relation to it. The law requires auditors to follow certain professional standards in their work. I'll introduce you to specific standards as and when they become relevant, but in this chapter I set out some practical matters that auditors must do and be aware of in order to carry out proper audits. The topics covered are:

✍ An audit

✍ Duties and rights of auditors

✍ Liability of auditors

✍ Audit failure

✍ Professional standards

✍ Professional behaviour

✍ Audit documentation

AN AUDIT

What is an audit?

An AUDIT is an exercise carried out by auditors to ascertain whether the financial statements prepared by the directors are properly prepared in accordance with an applicable financial reporting framework, (in the UK) in accordance with the Companies Act and give what is known as a true and fair view. The auditors issue an auditor's report (see below) which states whether this is the case or not.

Although the law states that an audit must be undertaken to see if the financial statements give a 'true and fair view', the law does not define what is meant by a true and fair view. This means that it is left to the courts to decide what it means on an individual basis, if the client or other parties dispute whether a proper audit was carried out (see below).

There are some generally recognised definitions of true and fair which auditors usually use.

TRUE is generally given to mean that information is factual and conforms with reality; that it is not false.

FAIR is generally given to mean that information is free from discrimination and bias and is in compliance with expected standards and rules.

Reasonable assurance and limitations of auditing

ISA 200 *Overall Objectives of the Independent Auditor and the Conduct of an Audit in Accordance With International Standards on Auditing* requires auditors to obtain REASONABLE ASSURANCE that the financial statements are free from material misstatement. Reasonable assurance is a high level of assurance, but not absolute. An auditor can never give absolute assurance because of the limitations of audits. The limitations of audit include:

- The fact that the directors make subjective judgements in preparing the financial statements and there are instances where a range of values could be acceptable

- The fact that the directors might not provide the auditors with all the information they need, either intentionally or unintentionally

- The fact that fraud may be being concealed, even by falsifying documents which might reasonably appear genuine

- The auditor tests on a sample basis, it is impractical and not cost effective to do otherwise, but evidence gained in this manner is persuasive, not conclusive

Appointment of auditors

Auditors are usually appointed by the shareholders at a shareholders' annual general meeting. In unusual circumstances, they may be appointed by directors. Auditors are usually re-elected annually, but in a private (Ltd) company, the existing auditors are automatically re-elected annually, unless the members remove them or they resign.

Later, we will examine the tests and judgements that comprise the audit exercise but first, we will look at the end product of the audit, the auditor's report to the shareholders.

Auditor's reports

The law requires that the auditor's report contains the name of the audit firm and is signed in the name of the senior statutory auditor on behalf of the firm. The senior statutory auditor is the engagement partner (see Chapter 6).

Professional standards give many more requirements for what an auditor's report must contain. I'll show you this in more detail when we get towards the end of some audits.

HOW IT WORKS

To illustrate where we are going, here is an example auditor's report for one of the firm's clients.

Independent auditors' report to the members of Rosalee Limited

We have audited the financial statements of Rosalee Limited for the year ended 30 April 2009 which comprise the profit and loss account, the balance sheet, the cash flow statement, the statement of total recognised gains and losses and the related notes. The financial reporting framework that has been applied in their preparation is applicable law and United Kingdom Accounting Standards (UK Generally Accepted Accounting Practice).

Respective responsibilities of directors and auditors

As explained more fully in the Statement of Directors' Responsibilities, the directors are responsible for the preparation of the financial statements and being satisfied that they give a true and fair view. Our responsibility is to audit the financial statements in accordance with applicable law and International Standards on Auditing (UK and Ireland). Those standards require us to comply with the Auditing Practices Board's Ethical Standards for auditors.

Scope of the audit of the financial statements

An audit involves obtaining evidence about the amounts and disclosures in the financial statements sufficient to give reasonable assurance that the financial statements are free from material misstatement, whether caused by fraud or error. This includes an assessment of: whether the accounting policies are appropriate to the company's circumstances and have been consistently applied and adequately disclosed; the reasonableness of significant accounting estimates made by the directors; and the overall presentation of the financial statements.

In addition, we read all the financial and non-financial information in the annual report to identify material inconsistencies with the audited financial statements. If we become aware of any apparent material misstatements or inconsistencies we consider the implications for our report.

Opinion

In our opinion the financial statements:

- Give a true and fair view of the state of the company affairs as at 30 April 2009 and its profit for the year then ended
- Have been properly prepared in accordance with United Kingdom Generally Accepted Accounting Practice
- Have been prepared in accordance with the Companies Act 2006.

Opinion on other matter prescribed by Companies Act 2006

In our opinion the information given in the Directors' Report for the financial year for which the financial statements are prepared is consistent with the financial statements.

Matters on which we are required to report by exception

We have nothing to report in respect of the following matters where the Companies Act 2006 requires us to report to you if, in our opinion:

- adequate accounting records have not been kept, or returns adequate for our audit have not been received from branches not visited by us; or
- the financial statements are not in agreement with the accounting records and returns; or
- certain disclosures of directors' remuneration specified by law are not made; or
- we have not received all the information and explanations we require for our audit.

(Signature)

(Senior Statutory auditor)

for and on behalf of Mason and Co, Statutory Auditors
Date

Task 1

Which of the following is not a limitation of auditing?

Directors may knowingly give auditors false information. ☐

Directors may give auditors false information by mistake. ☐

Audit evidence is conclusive not persuasive. ☐

Auditors use samples to obtain audit evidence. ☐

Task 2

Complete the following definitions: by filling in the gaps using the items in the pick list below.

.... is generally given to mean that .... is factual and conforms with reality: it is not ....

.... is generally given to mean that information is free from .... and .... and is in compliance with expected .... and ....

Pick list

Information

Bias

True

Discrimination

Fair

False

Rules

Standards

Internal audit

You may be familiar with the term internal audit. INTERNAL AUDIT is an appraisal activity established within an entity as a service to the entity. Its functions include, amongst other things, monitoring internal controls. In the course of work as an external auditor, you may come across internal audit in the companies you audit. Internal audit is an important control of the business, so we consider its role briefly in Chapter 3.

DUTIES AND RIGHTS OF AUDITORS

Duties

The main duty of the auditors in the UK is to give an opinion on the truth and fairness and proper preparation of the financial statements. They are also required to state that the directors' report is consistent with the financial statements.

The Companies Act requires that when auditors are carrying out their audit, they must ensure that the directors have maintained adequate accounting records and whether the financial statements agree with the underlying accounting records.

The auditors will state in their report if they discover:

- Adequate accounting records have not been kept

- Proper returns adequate for the audit have not been received from branches of the business not visited by the auditors

- The individual accounts are not in agreement with the accounting records

They will also state in their report if the directors and other staff have not given them sufficient information for the purposes of their audit.

Rights

The Companies Act gives auditors a number of legal rights in relation to their audit. These are:

- A right of access at all times to the company's books, accounts and vouchers

- A right to require such information and explanations from company officers as the auditors think necessary for the audit

If an officer of the company knowingly or recklessly gives the auditors a false or deceptive statement he is guilty of a criminal offence.

Auditors are also entitled to be given notice of meetings of the company's shareholders, are entitled to attend and speak at those meetings on matters that are relevant to them as auditors.

Task 3

Set out the rights and duties that auditors are given by the law.

LIABILITY OF AUDITORS

As already stated, the audit is an exercise carried out for the benefit of the shareholders of a company, as it is addressed to them. It enhances the confidence of users that the directors have put together financial statements that are free from material misstatement.

Negligence

If the auditors give a poor service, that is, if they perform an audit that is of substandard quality (for example, which states there are no material misstatements in the financial statements when that is not in fact the case), they may be liable to the shareholders as a result. Performing a poor quality audit may constitute negligence under English law, which is a matter for the courts to decide.

The term NEGLIGENCE refers to the way in which a service is carried out, that is carelessly, or to the legal wrong which arises when a person breaks a legal duty of care that is owed to another and causes loss to that other.

For negligence to be proven, three separate things must be established:

(1) The fact that a duty of care existed
(2) The fact that this duty of care was breached
(3) That fact that this caused loss to the claimant

Duty of care

Under English law, auditors owe a duty of care to their client. This is a implied into their **contract**, and cannot be disputed. Therefore, in negligence cases, if the claimant is the client with whom the audit firm have a contract, fact (1) above needs no further proof.

However, this is slightly complicated for auditors by the question of who the client is.

Who is the client?

We have noted above that the audit is conducted for the benefit of shareholders.

However, in English law, the shareholders of a company are often not considered in isolation, that is, as individuals, but as a single body. In that context, the shareholders are described as being the company.

HOW IT WORKS

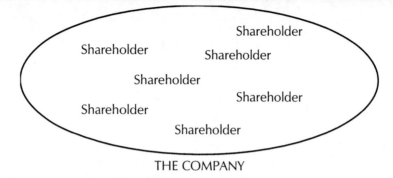

THE COMPANY

It is the **body of shareholders**, known as the company, that is considered to be the client for the purposes of negligence in audit.

When the body of shareholders (the company) as a whole sues for negligence, fact (1) above does not have to be proven.

The situation is different if an individual shareholder or another third party sues for negligence.

Other parties or individual shareholders

The audit is primarily carried out for the shareholders. However, many other parties may be interested in the financial statements of a company.

In most companies, the following may be interested:

- The **bank** (often a major lender to the company)
- **Suppliers** (who may extend credit to the company)
- **Customers** (who rely on the company to provide a quality service)
- **Employees** (who rely on the company for income)
- **Tax authorities** (who want to levy the correct tax from the company)
- If the company is public limited, **potential investors** (who are considering whether to invest in the company)

While all of these parties may be interested in the audited financial statements, it is important to remember that the audit is not carried out for them. They are certainly not the client, and English law has historically substantially restricted the chances of these parties proving negligence against the auditors.

One reason for this is that, in the case of these parties and individual shareholders, the auditor does not automatically owe them a duty of care, and they would have to prove that one existed.

The way that a duty of care might exist is if these parties have constructed a relationship with the auditors, for example by warning them that they believe a duty of care exists, or by telling them they are relying on the audited financial statements for a special purpose.

However, even then it is not automatic, and the auditors may be able to disclaim liability to these parties and say that a duty of care did not exist. Then the courts will have to decide whether such a duty did exist, examining the facts.

Breach of duty of care

For all parties, not only does a duty of care have to exist, but the claimant must prove that this duty was breached.

Again, this is a matter for the courts to determine when presented with the facts. However, there are some generally accepted principles about auditing which may indicate whether a duty of care has been met or breached.

For example, it is generally accepted that auditors will conduct audits according to professional standards. We shall look at what these professional standards are soon. You should bear in mind that if an audit firm does not carry out audits according to these professional standards, it may make it easier for disgruntled parties to prove negligence against the firm.

Loss caused

This is the third item that needs proving in a case of negligence. The claimant will not only have to show that he has suffered a loss, usually a financial loss, but that the loss was as a result of the breach of the duty of care on the part of the auditors. Again, this will be determined by the courts. If the auditors are found to have been negligent, they may have to pay financial reparation (known as damages) to the claimant.

Task 4

To whom might auditors owe a duty of care?

Please choose the appropriate option in each case.

	Options
■ Company	Automatic
	Must be proved
	Never
■ Bank	Automatic
	Must be proved
	Never
■ Individual shareholder	Automatic
	Must be proved
	Never
■ Creditor	Automatic
	Must be proved
	Never

AUDIT FAILURE

Performing a poor quality audit resulting in the auditors being found guilty of negligence can be described as audit failure, which can, of course, have serious consequences for audit firms.

One such consequence has already been mentioned. A firm may have to pay out substantial damages to a claimant if it has been proven that the auditors were negligent. This would clearly adversely affect the audit firm, and may even cause it to cease to operate, if the damages were so sizeable as to bankrupt the firm.

Such a legal case against a firm would bring substantial bad publicity, impacting on the firm's ability to retain and engage clients in the future, even if they did continue in operation.

In addition, the recognised supervisory body of that audit firm might take disciplinary action against the firm and its partners which could result in its ability to conduct audits being suspended.

Restriction of liability

The Companies Act 2006 entitles auditors to negotiate liability limitation agreements with their clients. The effect of such agreements is to restrict the extent of the auditors' liability (the amount of damages to be paid) in the event that negligence is proved against them. This restriction may be a specified amount above which an auditor will not be liable (a liability cap) or an agreement that if there are other parties contributing to the loss and the damage, that the auditor will only be held liable for his portion of the damage (proportional liability).

There are other ways that auditors can restrict their liability. Many firms include a statement in their auditor's report specifically excluding liability to parties other than the shareholders. This is known as a Bannermann paragraph, after the legal case in which such a course of action was recommended for auditors to avoid liability to third parties.

Lastly, individual audit partners can limit their personal liability for the firm's debts from such matters by changing how the audit firm is legally formed.

Traditionally, audit firms have been partnerships, where each partner is liable for the debts of the firm jointly with the other partners. It is now possible to set up audit firms in different legal forms, such as a limited liability partnership (LLP), where the partners have limited liability in the same way that shareholders in a company do. There are some drawbacks to forming an LLP however, such as requirements for increased publicity, such as filing accounts with the Companies Registrar.

Professional indemnity insurance

Lastly, a firm may insure against professional liability by taking out professional indemnity insurance. In fact, many audit firms are required to by their recognised supervisory body in the public interest, so that a firm is found liable, the injured parties can be compensated.

PROFESSIONAL STANDARDS

As I've already told you, auditors must carry out audits in accordance with professional standards, or they risk breaching their duty of care to clients. So I'll explain here a little more about what those professional standards are.

The Auditing Practices Board (APB)

The AUDITING PRACTICES BOARD is an independent body that issues professional guidance for auditors in the UK to follow. It is a constituent body of the Financial Reporting Council (FRC). The FINANCIAL REPORTING COUNCIL is the independent regulator of accounting and auditing in the UK. The government has delegated responsibility for standard-setting and monitoring to the FRC.

The APB issues standards which set out audit objectives and requirements to follow when carrying out audits required by law. Some of these are quality control standards, some are ethical standards, and most of them are engagement standards. The APB issues engagement standards known as INTERNATIONAL STANDARDS ON AUDITING (UK AND IRELAND) (ISAs).

In addition, the APB issues Practice Notes, which assist auditors in applying engagement standards to specific industries or types of company (for example, small companies) and Bulletins, which contain guidance on new or emerging issues. Both of these types of guidance are good practice not mandatory.

The International Audit and Assurance Standards Board (IAASB)

The INTERNATIONAL AUDIT AND ASSURANCE STANDARDS BOARD (IAASB) is an independent body working with the International Federation of Accountants (IFAC) which sets international standards for auditing.

It is the International Standards on Auditing (ISAs) set by IAASB that the UK's APB has adopted as national requirements in the UK. The IAASB is committed to setting high quality standards for auditing and enabling convergence between national and international standards so that globally, the quality of auditing is increased and auditing practice becomes more uniform round the world, so that public confidence in the global auditing profession is improved.

New standards are researched and consulted on, then subjected to public debate. The resulting draft standards are exposed to the public for comment. Any comments arising are considered and acted upon if necessary. A new standard is then issued when, at least, two-thirds of IAASB's members approve it.

Quality control

International Quality Control Standard 1 (ISQC 1) is an important standard. It sets out requirements for quality control standards in an audit firm. Practitioners must ensure that they put policies and procedures in place to meet certain requirements, particularly to ensure that the firm:

- Meets ethical requirements
- Only accepts and continues to maintain clients appropriately
- Has sufficient, competent staff to carry out the necessary assignments
- Has strong leadership for quality within the firm
- Assigns staff correctly to engagements
- Performs engagements in a quality manner
- Monitors its systems of quality control to ensure they work efficiently and effectively

Establishing good quality control procedures is a key way of reducing audit failure, discussed above.

International Standards on Auditing (ISAs)

The ISAs contain objectives, requirements and application and other explanatory material to help an auditor obtain reasonable assurance. The auditor must follow the requirements of relevant ISAs and must also have an understanding of the whole text of an ISA to enable him to apply the requirements properly.

Ethical standards

The IAASB has also issued an ethical code, and the APB has issued Ethical Standards, which are mainly concerned with the **independence** and **objectivity** of auditors, the latter being a fundamental principle of external auditing. As stated in Chapter 1, auditors should be independent of the company and its directors so that they can give an objective opinion to the shareholders.

It is important that auditors protect their independence from the companies they audit. Many things can compromise this independence, and the auditors must be vigilant and set up safeguards against loss of independence.

> ## Task 5
>
> Set out any factors you can think of which may compromise independence from a company being audited.

You may have come up with different factors, but in general terms independence can be affected by:

- Self-interest (for example, when an audit firm becomes over-reliant on a client, for instance, due to the high level of fees or number of different services they provide them)

- Self-review (for example, when audit staff review work that they themselves have prepared for a client, for example, if the firm also prepares the management accounts or financial statements*)

- Familiarity (for example, when audit staff have close personal relationships with client staff, or have grown over-accustomed to the client because they have worked on the audit for so many years)

- Advocacy (for example, if the audit firm is an a position of defending the client in a legal situation)

- Intimidation (for example, if the audit firm is threatened with legal action by the client)

- Management (for example, if an auditor starts to take authority for management decisions at an audit client)

* Auditors are not allowed to produce financial statements for public limited companies at all.

PROFESSIONAL BEHAVIOUR

Two other important principles of auditing are confidentiality and professional courtesy.

Confidentiality

CONFIDENTIALITY is the auditors' duty to keep client affairs private. As auditors are entitled to obtain all information they consider relevant from a company, they are obviously in a position of trust. A company is likely to view the information it gives the auditors as sensitive and would prefer auditors not to share it with outside parties.

The general rule is that auditors must keep client information secret.

There are some exceptions to this rule, when an auditor may be required or allowed to make a disclosure of confidential information. For example, if the auditor suspects the client of taking part in money laundering activities, he has a legal duty to disclose his suspicions to the firm's money laundering reporting officer (MLRO), who will in turn, report it to the Serious Organised Crime Agency (SOCA). The client may be breaching other laws which give the auditor a legal duty to report them to the appropriate statutory authority, although if the breaches result in money laundering offences, they must be careful not to alert the client to criminal investigation of money laundering. Such alerting is itself a criminal offence known as 'tipping-off'. Examples of money laundering offences include:

- Offences that indicate dishonest behaviour – such as tax evasion or not returning overpayments by customers (where the client has attempted but failed to return such overpayments, dishonesty is not indicated)

- Offences that involve saved costs (such as where a company is saving money by not complying with environmental law, for example, by dumping waste illegally rather than paying a company to remove it)

- Conduct overseas that would be illegal in the UK, for example, bribery of government officials

However, if the police question an auditor in the course of normal enquiries about a company, the auditor must be very careful not to breach his duty of confidentiality unless he is very sure he has a legal duty to do so. He should seek legal advice when put in such a position.

In terms of voluntary disclosures, the auditor is entitled to make disclosures in a legal case where it is necessary for the purposes of defending himself.

Security

In practice, security measures by the auditor may be a very important part of keeping the duty of confidentiality.

Task 6

Set out any security measures an auditor might have to take to ensure he does not breach his duty of confidentiality.

Security falls into two categories.

First, auditors must be very careful in carrying out their work that they do not discuss their work in inappropriate places. This may be the case both at the client and outside the client's premises.

For example, the directors may tell the auditors information that they don't want the rest of the client staff to know. The auditors should only discuss such information when they know other client staff members cannot overhear them.

For this reason it is very important that the client provides the auditors with a suitable place to work when they are carrying out work at a client's premises. They should be given a private room rather than being asked to work in the middle of the accounts' department.

The auditors must be careful in discussing client information away from the client premises.

Task 7

From the following list, identify where it may be appropriate to discuss client information and where it would not be so appropriate:

Audit firm premises ☐

Accounts department at client premises ☐

Private meeting room at client premises ☐

During lunch at restaurant local to client premises ☐

During lunch at restaurant distant from client premises ☐

There are many places where it is inappropriate to discuss client information. The general rule is that client information should not be discussed in a public place or with anyone outside of the audit firm.

Second, auditors must ensure that the security arrangements over their physical work are sufficient. We look at the types of files of work that auditors compile in the next section, but for now, you must remember that these files and any computers storing audit work must be kept secure. Auditors are often issued with lockable cases by their firm so that they can lock audit files away when they are not in use and can be transported securely.

This may mean not leaving the office auditors are using at the client open if the auditors are not there, not leaving client files in the auditor's car, and ensuring that the storage facilities for client files at the auditor's own office are secure. If older files are put away in storage, this should be locked with only the auditors having access to it.

Professional courtesy

Another important concern is that of courtesy. Auditors are entitled to obtain information and explanations from client staff, as we have already discussed.

However, we should bear in mind that the business of the company does not stop or 'freeze' just because the auditors are in, so members of the client's staff are attempting to do their everyday jobs as well as assist the auditors in any way that they can. Auditors should be mindful of this and be as courteous and considerate as possible.

Task 8

Albert, an auditor, finished work at the client for the day and is taking work home with him to finish off in the evening. The files are on the back seat of his car. On the way home, he parks in the street outside the local shop and takes five minutes to buy some essential groceries.

Beth, an auditor, is part of a team of auditors at a client's premises. They have been allocated a room to work in, for which a senior member of the audit team has a key. The rest of Beth's team are carrying out work at different places on the site. As she needs to obtain some information from the accounts department, she locks the audit files left in the room in her lockable case before leaving the room.

Clare and Daniel, two members of an audit team, have gone from a client to a local pub for lunch. Daniel is telling Clare what audit work he wants her to carry out in the afternoon, with substantial reference to the client's operations.

Edwards Auditors Co, an audit firm, has insufficient storage facilities at its premises to maintain all the historic audit files that need to be retained for quality control purposes. It invests in a storage room in a large storage facility. The storage room is unlocked by using a code known only to staff of Edwards Auditors Co.

Task

Comment on the security in each of the above situations.

AUDIT DOCUMENTATION

I've mentioned audit files when setting out the security measures that auditors must take. I will now introduce you to audit files and the working papers they contain within them, to enable you to carry out any audit procedures to a proper standard from the beginning.

Working papers

Auditors document the work they do in working papers. WORKING PAPERS are the material prepared by and for, or, obtained and retained by, the auditor, in connection with the performance of the audit. They provide a record of the audit procedures performed, relevant audit evidence obtained and conclusions reached. They contain evidence which provides the basis for the auditor's opinion and also provide evidence that the audit has been carried out in accordance with ISAs. They may be in the form of data stored on paper, film, electronic media or other media.

The documentation serves other purposes, such as:

- Assisting the audit team to plan and perform the audit
- Allowing more senior members of the team to check junior members' work
- Enabling the team to be accountable for its work
- Retaining a record of matters of continuing significance
- Allowing quality control review
- Enabling external inspections if necessary

Auditors usually reference working papers with a number of details:

- Name (or initials) of the auditor who prepared the working paper
- Date the working paper was prepared
- Area of the audit being worked on (for example, inventory)
- Identifying characteristics of the item/matters being tested
- Year-end of the financial statements being audited

Working papers are reviewed by a member of staff more senior than the one that prepared them. When a working paper is reviewed, the reviewer also initials the working paper and dates when it was reviewed.

Document what?

The engagement standard relating to working papers sets out what auditors must document in a general rule:

'The auditor shall prepare audit documentation on a timely basis. The auditor shall prepare audit documentation that is sufficient to enable an experienced auditor, having no previous connection with the audit, to understand the **nature, timing and extent of the audit procedures** performed to comply with the ISAs and applicable legal and regulatory requirements, the **results** of the audit procedures performed, and the **audit evidence obtained**; and **significant matters** arising during the audit, the **conclusions reached** thereon, and **significant professional judgements** made in reaching those conclusions.'

This includes information on:

- Planning the audit
- The nature, timing and extent of the audit procedures performed
- Results of the audit procedures and the audit evidence obtained
- Conclusions drawn from audit evidence obtained from procedures
- Any contentious issues and how they were resolved
- Discussions on significant matters had with client staff/officers

We examine all these aspects of an audit later on, when I introduce you to some real clients and we get on with some audit work.

Auditors must document their reasoning on significant matters where they have exercised judgement and the conclusions they have drawn.

HOW IT WORKS

Here is an example of a working paper on payables (creditors) from a client I have worked on in the past:

Client: _The HEC Ltd_		Prepared by	Review ed by
		........_PC_...........	....
Subject: _Payables_			
		Date: **16.2.X8**	Date:...............
Year end: _31 December 20X7_			

H³/₁

Work done									
	Selected a sample of trade payables as at 31 December and reconciled the supplier's statement to the								
	year end purchase ledger balance. Vouched any reconciling items to source documentation.								
Results	See H³/₂								
	One credit note, relating to Ambrosia Ltd. has not been accounted for. An adjustment is required.								
	DEBIT	Trade payables		£1,327					
	CREDIT	Purchases			£1,327 H1/2				
	One other error was found, which was immaterial, and which was the fault of the supplier.								
	In view of the error found, however, we should recommend that the client management checks								
	supplier statement reconciliations at least on the larger accounts. Management letter point.								
Conclusion									
	After making the adjustment noted above, purchased ledger balances are fairly stated								
	as at 31 December 20X7								

Document how much?

The ISA suggests that the auditor should write down enough that an experienced auditor who has no experience of the particular client could follow and understand what had been done.

The form, content and extent of audit documentation will depend on factors such as:

- The nature of the audit procedures
- Risks of material misstatement
- The extent of judgement required
- The significance of the evidence
- The nature and extent of exceptions identified

In other words, the auditor will need to use his judgement in making this decision.

Standardisation of working papers

There may be cases where working papers, for example, checklists or specimen letters, are standardised, so that the auditor merely has to complete the client details. However, the auditor must always take care when using standardised working papers, as it is never appropriate to take a mechanical approach to auditing, audit judgement must always be exercised.

Audit files

Working papers usually include:

- Information about the entity and its environment
- Evidence of the audit planning process
- Evidence of the auditor's consideration of the internal audit function (if relevant)
- Analyses of transactions and balances in the financial statements
- Analyses of significant ratios and trends
- Identified and assessed risks of material misstatements
- Record of the nature, timing and extent of resulting procedures
- Copies of letters concerning matters communicated to, or discussed with, management such as the terms of the engagement
- Conclusions reached by the auditor on significant aspects of the audit
- Copies of the financial statements and auditor's report

For one audit, this can amount to a lot of working papers! Working papers are therefore contained in **audit files**, as I stated above in the context of security.

Audit regulations require that working papers must be kept for at least six years from the end of the accounting period to which they relate.

Review

Working papers produced by audit staff are reviewed by more senior staff. Matters to consider when performing a review:

- Whether the work has been performed in accordance with the audit plan
- Firm procedures
- The overall audit strategy
- The work is adequate in the light of results and has been sufficiently documented

- Whether there is a need to revise the nature, timing and extent of work performed
- Whether significant matters have been raised for further consideration
- Whether appropriate consultations have taken place and been documented
- Whether the objectives of the audit procedure have been achieved
- Whether the conclusions are consistent with the results of the work performed

When the audit work has been completed and reviewed, the audit engagement partner completes an overall review of the working papers to ensure that he is able to issue his opinion.

When a review takes place, the reviewer will often use a separate working paper to record queries and their answer.

Client: *The HEC Ltd*	Prepared by	Review ed by	
	PC	*TB*	*1/3*
Subject: *Manager review*			
Year end: *Y/E 31 December 20X7*	Date: *16.2.X8*	Date:	

1 Have the non-current asset balances been		*Yes – see working papers*			*F1*	*PC*
agreed to the non-current asset register and						*TB*
nominal ledgers?						

The need to sign off all working papers and queries acts as an extra check, helping to ensure that all work has been carried out and completed.

After the senior/supervisor has reviewed the work of the assistants there will usually be a **manager review**, which will cover some of the assistants' work, all of the senior/supervisor's work and an overall review of the audit work. Then there will be an **engagement partner review**, which examines the manager's review, any controversial areas of the audit, the auditors' report and such like.

CHAPTER OVERVIEW

- An audit is an exercise on the financial statements to see whether they give a true and fair view

- The auditors' key duties are to report on truth and fairness and proper preparation of the financial statements

- However, they must in addition report if they discover accounting records are not kept and on a number of other issues

- Auditors are given a number of rights by the Companies Act

- The auditors may be liable to the client or other parties if they carry out a negligent audit

- Three things must be proven in the case of negligent audit:

    - A duty of care existed
    - It was breached
    - Loss resulted

- An auditor always has a duty of care to the client (the shareholders as a body)

- Auditors must follow professional standards set by the Auditing Practices Board/International Audit and Assurance Standards Board

- Engagement standards issued by the APB are known as ISAs

- Auditors must behave in a certain way as well. They should keep client affairs secret and deal with staff courteously

- Security over audit work is a key issue in confidentiality

- Audit work is documented in working papers, which are maintained in audit files

- Work performed by audit staff is reviewed by more senior staff

Keywords

Audit – an exercise carried out by auditors to ascertain whether the financial statements prepared by the directors are properly prepared in accordance with an applicable financial reporting framework, (in the UK) in accordance with the Companies Act and give what is known as a true and fair view

True – generally given to mean that information is factual and conforms with reality; that it is not false

Fair – generally given to mean that information is free from discrimination and bias and is in compliance with expected standards and rules

Reasonable assurance – a high level of assurance, but not absolute. An auditor can never give absolute assurance because of the limitations of audits

Internal Audit – appraisal activity within an organisation to monitor internal controls

Negligence – refers to the way in which a service is carried out, that is carelessly, or to the legal wrong which arises when a person breaks a legal duty of care that is owed to another and causes loss to that other

The **Auditing Practices Board** – an independent body that issues professional guidance for auditors to follow

The **Financial Reporting Council** – the independent regulator of accounting and auditing in the UK

The **International Audit and Assurance Standards Board** – an independent body working with the International Federation of Accountants (IFAC) which sets international standards for auditing

International Standards on Auditing (UK and Ireland) – engagement standards issued by the APB

Confidentiality – the auditors' duty to keep client affairs private

Working papers – the material prepared by and for, or, obtained and retained by, the auditor in connection with the performance of the audit

TEST YOUR LEARNING

Test 1 You are required to complete the following definition of an audit by filling in the gaps using the items in the pick list below.

An .... is an exercise carried out by .... to ascertain whether the .... prepared by the .... are (in the UK) in accordance with the UK Gaap and the .... and give what is known as a

....

Pick list

Statements

Audit

Directors

True and fair view

Companies Act 2006

Financial

Auditors

Test 2 State whether the following statements are True or False in respect of external auditors' duties and rights.

	Options
Auditors are required to report on the truth and fairness of financial statements.	True
	False
Auditors have a right of access to a company's books and records at any time.	True
	False
Auditors are entitled to obtain explanations from the officers of a company.	True
	False

Test 3 Which one of the following best describes to whom the auditors owe a duty of care?

Auditors owe a duty of care to:

All users of financial statements ☐

The client (that is, the company, comprising all the shareholders) ☐

Shareholders ☐

The client and any other parties with whom they have implied a special relationship ☐

Test 4 What three things need to be proven in a case for negligence?

Test 5 Set out the guidance issued by the APB.

Test 6 You are required to complete the following definition of confidentiality by filling in the gaps using the items in the pick list below.

.... is the duty to keep .... affairs ....

Pick list

Client

Private

Confidentiality

Test 7 Set out why security procedures are important to auditors.

Test 8 Set out what working papers are.

chapter 3:
THE COMPANY ENVIRONMENT (CONTROLS)

— chapter coverage 📖 —

In this chapter, I introduce you to the environment of the company. Professional standards require auditors to obtain an understanding of the entity and its environment, which includes its internal control systems. We'll look at the procedures auditors carry out to do this later, but for now, examine what an internal control system is, and the types of common controls you can expect to come across when auditing. The topics covered are:

✎ Internal control systems

✎ Sales systems

✎ Purchases systems

✎ Payroll systems

✎ Non-current asset systems

✎ Inventory systems

INTERNAL CONTROL SYSTEMS

INTERNAL CONTROL is the process designed, implemented and maintained by those charged with governance (the directors), management, and other personnel, to provide reasonable assurance about the achievement of the entity's objectives with regard to the reliability of financial reporting, effectiveness and efficiency of operations and compliance with applicable laws and regulations. The term 'controls' refers to aspects of one or more of the components of internal control.

HOW IT WORKS

Put another way:

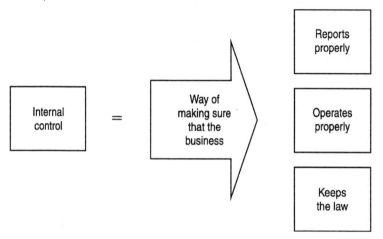

Internal control is designed and implemented to address risks that these aims of a company will not be met. Such risks are known as business risks. BUSINESS RISK is the risk that the company will not meet its objectives.

A system of internal control has various elements, and I'll talk you through each of these elements. The elements set out in ISA 315 *Identifying and Assessing the Risks of Material Misstatement Through Understanding the Entity and its Environment* are:

- The control environment
- The entity's risk assessment process
- The information system
- Control activities
- Monitoring of controls

Control environment

The CONTROL ENVIRONMENT is the **attitudes**, **awareness** and **actions** of management and those charged with governance regarding internal control and its importance.

In other words, control environment is the foundation on which any internal control system rests. The directors can have many activities to ensure that nothing goes wrong in their company, but if everyone ignores them, and the directors do nothing about that, then the internal control system is not likely to operate very well.

The opposite can be true – if the directors really care about internal controls, but their actual control activities are unsatisfactory, it doesn't matter how much they care, the internal control system is likely to be substandard.

However, a good control environment usually means a good internal control system overall.

There are various ways that a good control environment can be seen in practice:

- Directors communicate and enforce integrity and ethical values
- Directors and staff are committed to competence
- Directors participate in control activities
- Management operates in a way that promotes control
- The organisation is structured in a way that promotes control
- Authority and responsibility for controls is assigned to people
- Human resources policies promote controls

A bad control environment can be seen when the opposite of some of these is true, for example:

- Directors circumvent and ignore controls to get things done

Task 1

An external auditor is required to obtain an understanding of the control environment within an audited entity.

Select whether the following factors contribute to a strong control environment or a weak control environment.

	Options
Management prefer favourable to honest reporting within the business.	Strong Weak
Management take the lead in enforcing control values.	Strong Weak

Size of company

The size of a company will have an impact on the control environment.

> ## Task 2
>
> Set out ways in which you think the control environment is affected by the size of a company.

Entity's risk assessment process

As we noted above, the internal control system is all about responding to risks that may affect the company's objectives being met. The three key objectives were shown in the diagram above – reporting properly, operating properly and keeping the law. Different companies may be affected by different risks in achieving these basic objectives.

HOW IT WORKS

I've already mentioned the Heavenly Eating Company Limited (HEC). I worked on the audit last year. It is a small company with three directors, two of whom work in the business. It operates a chain of three organic food shops and also has a number of customers to whom it delivers on account. By way of example, I can tell you that HEC has the following risks with regard to the three identified business objectives:

(1) **Reporting properly** – none of the directors has any accounting experience.

(2) **Operating properly** – the business has three sites, and there are only two working directors, so they cannot oversee all the operations all the time.

   In addition, the business is heavily reliant on the directors, and if they become ill or incapacitated, the operations of the business will come under threat.

(3) **Keeping the law** – the business sells food, which is a heavily regulated business, but the directors are not legal experts in this area.

These are not the only business risks HEC faces.

All entities will have some sort of process (not necessarily formal) for assessing the risks a company faces and then implementing strategies (controls) to mitigate the risks.

HOW IT WORKS

Going back to the risks identified at the HEC, I can show you what actions the directors have taken in respect of the risks:

(1) None of the directors has any accounting experience, so they use the services of a local accountant to keep the accounting records and produce financial statements.

(2) The business has three sites but only two working directors, but the directors ensure that they visit the sites they are not based at regularly and communicate operating policies to the managers of those shops.

The business is heavily reliant on the operating directors, but they keep each other informed as to their actions and intentions and also involve other staff members in the work that they do, so that if one of them is incapacitated, the other staff members could perform their function.

(3) The directors are not legal experts, but subscribe to a legal journal covering food and hygiene law to ensure that they remain aware of important new issues in the law.

Size and type of company

Clearly, the risks facing a business will be different company by company and will also be affected by whether a company is large or small, whether it operates in a highly regulated industry or not.

In terms of financial reporting risk, the most important risk for the purposes of auditors, is that there could be various relevant factors to take into consideration.

For example, the announcement of new accounting standards will affect different companies in different ways.

A company with a finance department is probably at less risk than a company without one, but if that department is subject to high staff turnover, then that can present an alternative risk.

A company that expands rapidly or diversifies into different business areas can have a high financial reporting risk whereas a company that continues to do what it has always done will have less risk.

In terms of risk assessment, it may be the case that a smaller company tackles this with the assistance of external advisers. For example, a small company may be reliant on the business advice that auditors may give in conjunction with their audit, whereas a larger company will rely more on internal staff and may even employ people specifically to assess risks to the business.

Task 3

I've already introduced you to one of the companies I'm going to use to show you how to implement audit procedures. Now I'm going to tell you a little about another of our audit clients, Metal Extrusions Midlands Limited.

Metal Extrusions Midlands Limited (MEM) is a family business which is 80 years old. It has six family members on the board of directors, four of whom are active in the business. It employs 50 staff, 40 in manufacturing, ten in administration, which includes a finance department with a staff of five, including a financial controller, who is not on the board of directors. She is a qualified accountant. None of the directors has any accounting skill.

MEM produces metal extrusions, which is a highly mechanised operation. It functions in one factory where it has always operated. The factory and its machinery are very old. MEM made a significant investment in new machinery in 1954. There have been few developments in metal extrusion since that time. However, the company has been experiencing competition in recent years from a new company set up by two disgruntled former employees.

MEM has several suppliers of metals and other materials required for production. There are two major suppliers, one of which is British and the other is French. The company purchases 30% of its metal raw materials from the French supplier, who insists on invoicing and being paid in Euros.

Task

Set out business risks you can identify, particularly with regard to the business objectives of (1) reporting properly (2) operating properly and (3) keeping the law.

Information system

An INFORMATION SYSTEM consists of infrastructure (physical and hardware components), software, people, procedures and data. The balance between these things depends on whether the information system is manual or computerised. Most companies now make at least some use of information technology (IT) in their information systems.

HOW IT WORKS: MANUAL SYSTEM

Here is an example of an information system with regard to purchases at HEC. (As the auditor I had to gain an understanding of how it captured and recorded information.)

Rosemary Philips is the director in charge of purchases and seeking new suppliers. She places an order with a supplier by telephoning them or under an existing written agreement. She keeps a record of all orders in the **order book**.

When goods are received by the company, they also receive a **purchase invoice**. Regardless of whom the invoice is given or sent to, all invoices are passed to Rosemary, or put in her **invoices received file**. Rosemary pays purchase invoices once a month. Any invoice she pays is marked with a P, and she enters the details of the cheque into a **cash book**.

Once a month, the accountant writes-up the **purchase ledger** from the invoices in the invoices received file and the cashbook. At the end of the year, the accountant extracts the balance from the purchase ledger into the **trial balance** in order to create the **financial statements**.

In this system, information is traced through from invoices to the financial statements. As it is a manual system, it is largely based on people, procedures and documents.

HOW IT WORKS: COMPUTERISED SYSTEM

By comparison, Peter Tyme, the sales director at HEC, has put together a combined manual and computerised system for credit sales.

He receives sales orders in a variety of ways: by telephone, by e-mail and in person. Whenever he receives an order, he notes it in the **sales order book**. Some orders can be fulfilled from shop stock, others must be ordered from suppliers.

When an order is delivered, Peter raises a **despatch note** on his computer. The computer automatically raises an **invoice** when a despatch note is raised. These documents are printed off and sent to the customer. When the documents are printed, the computer programme automatically updates the **sales day book** which is also on the computer.

When customers pay, Peter enters the details of the cheques into the **cash book**.

Once a month, the accountant writes-up the **sales ledger** from the sales day book and the cash book. Once a year, he extracts information from the sales ledger to the **trial balance** in order to produce the financial statements.

Size of company

The larger the company, the more complex it is likely that its information system will become. It is also likely that large companies will have computerised, rather than manual systems.

Control activities

CONTROL ACTIVITIES are the policies and procedures that help ensure that management directives are carried out (they are often simply known as controls).

There are a variety of control activities that can be used by an organisation:

- Performance reviews – comparing budgets to actual performance.

- Information processing – checking that transactions have been processed accurately, completely and have been authorised.

- Physical controls – controls over the physical security of assets.

- Segregation of duties – making sure that a number of people are involved in recording each transaction to minimise opportunity for fraud and error.

What the actual activity is will depend on the business and its risks. However, there are some common control activities that are used in many companies, and we look at these in more detail when we study specific accounting areas of the business later in the chapter.

HOW IT WORKS

Control activities may include the following:

Authorisation of documents

Transactions should be **authorised** by an appropriate person, for example, overtime should be authorised by departmental heads.

Controls over computerised applications

These may be general controls (see below) or application controls which may be built into the computer (see below).

Controls over arithmetical accuracy

For example, when invoices are raised or received, a staff member should ensure that the invoice adds up correctly.

Maintaining control accounts and trial balances

You should know from your accounting studies that these can be useful in ensuring mistakes have not been made in financial records, for example, some errors will result in a trial balance not balancing.

Reconciliations

Reconciling two different sources of information, such as a bank statement and a cashbook, or a purchase ledger account and a statement from the supplier can also highlight if errors have occurred.

Such a reconciliation may also be comparing an external source of information with an internal source of information – another useful control on whether the internal source is correct.

Comparing assets to records

Again, this helps show if errors have been made in recording. For example, staff might compare non-current assets to what is recorded in the non-current asset register or cash in the petty cash tin to what is in the petty cash book.

Restricting access (physical controls)

A good way of restricting errors and particularly fraud or theft is to restrict access to assets – for example, by locking receipts in a safe until they go to the bank, having codes to unlock the cash tills, locking the stores where inventory is kept.

Application computer controls

APPLICATION CONTROLS are controls relating to the transactions and standing data relevant to each computer-based accounting system and are specific to each such application.

Controls can be found over **input** to the computer (covering completeness, accuracy and authorisation) **processing** and **standing data**.

HOW IT WORKS

Items being input are subject to tests (both manual and programmed):

For completeness, the inputter might check processed output to source documents on a one-to-one basis, or might check the number of transactions posted with the number of original documents. There may be an agreement of the total value of the amount processed (a batch total) between the source documents and the total input to the computer.

For accuracy, the computer may have programmed controls to check the plausibility of information being entered into certain fields. For example, some fields might be wrong if they were a negative number, or the VAT field might have to be a sensible percentage (20% or 5%) of the total field. Invoice numbers might have to have a letter as well as number values to be valid. Scrutinising output also helps to check accuracy.

Checks over authorisation are manual – monitoring to see if the source documentation input has been evidenced as authorised by suitable personnel.

Controls over processing will be similar to the above. In addition, there may be a control built into a programme that warns the user if they try to log out before processing is finished.

Controls over standing data will involve regular reviews of the data to ensure that it is correct and items such as hash totals (for example, number of personnel on the payroll) ensure no unauthorised amendments have been made.

General computer controls

GENERAL IT CONTROLS are controls other than application controls relating to the computer environment. They aim to establish a framework of overall supervision over the computer information system's activities to provide a reasonable level of assurance that the overall objectives of internal controls are achieved.

Controls will exist over developing computer applications, preventing unauthorised changes to applications, testing genuine changes when they are made, and preventing applications being used by the wrong people at the wrong time.

HOW IT WORKS

General IT controls include matters of security – limiting access to computers or computer programmes, both physically (by locking them up) and by using passwords, creating backups of important files and keeping them secure – and procedures over development and testing – isolating development and testing, obtaining approval.

Segregation of duties is also an important general control over computers – as other users of the same programmes will notice any unauthorised changes.

Size of company

Control activities are likely to be similar, regardless of the size of the company. However, who is involved in carrying out control activities may vary. I have already mentioned in the context of control environment that in smaller companies, those charged with governance (directors) may be more involved in actually implementing control activities.

Segregation of duties can be a serious problem for small companies, where often there are insufficient staff to allow proper segregation between duties to occur.

Task 4

Look back to the descriptions of the information systems at HEC. Comment on the degree of segregation of duties operating in these systems.

Monitoring of controls

MONITORING OF CONTROLS is a process to assess the quality of internal control performance over time.

In many entities, this is performed by the internal audit function. If there is no internal audit function, it would be done as a matter of course by departmental heads – for example, the sales director is likely to become aware of deficiencies of controls in the sales cycle because it means his department does not operate as well as it might.

Size of company

Who monitors is likely to be affected by the size of the company. For example, a small company is unlikely to have an internal audit function. Monitoring of controls is likely to be less formal in a smaller entity too.

Limitations of internal control systems

However good any single element of an internal control system (discussed above), an internal control system can never be perfect, due to inherent limitations.

The key limiting factors are that people make mistakes and may not operate controls properly and also that people can deliberately work around control systems if they want to defraud the company, especially if more than one person is involved. In addition, the directors may have missed important matters when designing the systems or designed controls badly, so that they do not achieve objectives.

SALES SYSTEMS

I've talked about internal controls at some length. Now we are going to look at the types of controls that are found in sales systems and the reasons that they are set up (their objectives, that is, the risks they are designed to mitigate).

Control objectives in the sales system

Task 5

Think for a moment about what the aims of an internal control system over sales might be, and what risks it might be aiming to mitigate. In doing so, you might find it helpful to think through the stages of the sales process. When you have thought it through, read the text below which sets out the answers.

Here we are focusing mainly on the risk of credit sales. When a company is making cash sales, no credit is granted, and often there is no formal order as the customer chooses and pays for goods which are readily available. Risks associated with cash sales are more in respect of the actual cash element which is discussed later.

Orders and extending credit

- A company should only supply goods to customers who are likely to pay for them (**risk** – the company loses goods of value and doesn't receive value in return). (This is often termed as the customer 'having a good credit rating'.)

- A company should encourage customers to pay promptly (**risk** – the company loses the value of being able to use the money in their business or interest on the money in the bank due to late payment).

- A company should record orders correctly (**risk** – the company sends the wrong goods to the customer causing added cost or risk of loss of the customer).

- A company should fulfil orders promptly/at all (**risk** – the company loses custom).

Despatching and invoicing goods

- A company should record all goods it sends out (**risk** – goods are sent out and not invoiced, and the company loses money).

- A company should invoice all goods and services sold correctly (**risk** – insufficient is charged and the company loses money).

- A company should only invoice goods it has sent out (**risk** – company charges for goods in error and loses custom).

- A company should only issue credit notes where required (**risk** – company issues credit notes incorrectly and loses money).

Recording and accounting for sales, credit control

- A company should record all invoiced sales in its accounting records (sales ledger and general ledger) (**risks** – sales are not recorded and wrongly omitted from financial statements, and payment is not chased as sale was never recorded).

- A company should record all credit notes in its accounting records (**risks** – as above, financial statements likely to be misstated and potential to lose custom by chasing cancelled debts).

- A company should record all invoiced sales in the correct sales ledger accounts (**risks** – losing custom by chasing the wrong customer for the debt and not receiving the money from the correct customer).

- A company must ensure that invoices are recorded in the sales ledger in the correct time period (**risk** – errors in the financial statements due to counting both the sale and the related inventory as assets or counting neither).

- A company must identify debts for which payment might be doubtful (**risks** – company fails to take action until it is too late to retrieve the debt and, in the worst case, company wrongly records irrecoverable receivables as assets in the financial statements).

Receiving payment (cash)

- A company should record all money received (**risks** – the money could be stolen or lost, custom could be lost through chasing payments already made by the customer, the financial statements are likely to be misstated).

- A company should bank all money received (**risks** – the money could be stolen or lost (with consequences as above), the company loses out on interest that could be being made on receipts).

- A company should safeguard money received in the period until it is banked (**risk** – money may be stolen in the interim period).

Task 6

For each of the objectives given in bullet points above, can you think of a procedure (a control activity) which will help achieve the objective? When you have thought it through, read the next section, which gives you some examples of controls.

Controls in the sales system

I'll list some examples of control procedures in the sales system relating to the objectives I outlined above, but before I do, I want to emphasise the importance of segregation of duties in a sales system.

Task 7

Which stages of the sales system do you feel ought to be dealt with by different staff members, and why? Read through the following text to see the answer.

It is possible that a staff member could create a false customer in order to steal the company's inventory and then not pay for it. This would only be possible if there was one person in charge of orders and credit control/sales ledgers.

There are two key potential frauds with regard to sales receipts. First, a staff member may intercept receipts when they arrive at the company and steal them before they are recorded. Second, a staff member may steal receipts and allocate receipts to the sales ledger records wrongly (in other words, make it look as if the customer is further behind in payment than he actually is on an ongoing basis). Such a fraud may not be discovered as the customer may never appear behind enough in payments to be chased for overdue debts.

In order to prevent such frauds, several people should be involved in dealing with cash receipts.

Other key control activities include the following:

Orders and extending credit

- Credit terms offered to customers should be authorised by senior personnel and reviewed regularly

- Credit checks should be run on new customers

- Changes in customer data (for example, their address) should be authorised by senior personnel

- Orders should only be accepted from customers with no existing payment problems

- Order documents should be sequentially numbered so that 'false sales' can be traced

Despatching and invoicing goods

- Despatch of goods should be authorised by appropriate personnel and checked back to order documents

- Despatched goods should be checked for quality and quantity

- Goods sent out should be recorded

- Records of sent out goods should be agreed to customer orders, despatch notes and invoices

- Despatch notes should be sequentially numbered and the sequence checked regularly

- Returned goods should be checked for quality

- Returned goods should be recorded on goods returned notes

- Customers should sign despatch notes as proof of receipt

- Invoices should be prepared using authorised prices and quantities and should be checked to despatch notes

- Invoices should be checked to ensure they add up correctly

- Credit notes should be authorised by appropriate personnel

- Invoices and credit notes should be pre-numbered and the sequence checked regularly

- Inventory records should be updated from goods sent out records

- Sales invoices should be matched with signed delivery notes and sales orders

- Orders not yet delivered should be regularly reviewed

Recording and accounting for sales, credit control

- Sales invoice sequence should be recorded and spoilt invoices recorded and destroyed

- Sales receipts should be matched with invoices

- Customer remittance advices should be retained

- Sales returns and price adjustments should be recorded separately from the original sale

- Procedures should exist to record sales in the correct period

- Receivable statements should be prepared regularly

- Receivable statements should be checked regularly

- Receivable statements should be safeguarded so they cannot be amended before they are sent out

- Overdue accounts should be reviewed and followed-up

- Write-off of irrecoverable receivables should be authorised by appropriate personnel

- The sales ledger control account should be reconciled regularly

- The sales ledger and profit margins should be analysed regularly

Receiving payment (cash)

- There should be safeguards to protect post received to avoid interception

- Two people should be present at post opening, a list of receipts should be made and post should be stamped with the date opened

- There should be restrictions on who is allowed to accept cash (cashiers or sales people)

- Cash received should be evidenced (till rolls, receipts)

- Cash registers should be regularly emptied

- Tills rolls should be reconciled to cash collections which should then be agreed to bankings

- Cash shortages should be investigated

- Cash records should be maintained promptly

- There should be appropriate arrangements made when cashiers are on holiday

- Receipts books should be serially numbered and kept locked up

- Bankings should be made daily

- Paying-in books should be compared to initial cash records

- All receipts should be banked together

- Opening of new bank accounts should be restricted and authorised

- Cash floats held should be limited

- There should be restrictions on making payments from cash received and restricted access to cash held on the premises

- Cash floats should be checked by an independent person sometimes on a surprise basis

- Cash should be locked up outside hours

Task 8

What are the objectives of the following control procedures?

- Credit checks should be run on new customers
- Sales invoices should be sequentially numbered
- Receivable statements should be prepared regularly
- Restrictions on who is allowed to receive cash

You should also run through the lists of controls given in the text above to ensure you follow the objectives behind each of them.

HOW IT WORKS

Here is the some of the information system relating to sales at HEC. You should recognise it as I outlined it earlier.

Peter receives sales orders in a variety of ways: by telephone, by e-mail and in person. Whenever he receives an order, he **notes it in the sales order book**. Some orders can be fulfilled from shop stock, others must be ordered from suppliers.

When an order is delivered, Peter **raises a despatch note** on his computer. The computer **automatically raises an invoice** when a despatch note is raised. These documents are printed off and sent to the customer. When the documents are printed, the **computer programme automatically updates the sales day book** which is also on the computer.

When customers pay, Peter **enters the details of the cheques into the cash book**.

Some of the control procedures in the system have been highlighted. Some of these are manual controls and others are computerised. For instance, orders are manually recorded in the order book, but sales invoices are automatically listed in the sales day book as a result of a computer programme.

Task 9

The system at HEC is very basic and far from perfect. Describe other controls that could exist in the system as outlined above.

PURCHASES SYSTEMS

Control objectives in the purchases system

Task 10

Think for a moment about what the aims of an internal control system over purchases might be, and what risks it is aiming to mitigate. In doing so, you might find it helpful to think through the stages of the purchases process. When you have thought it through, read the text below which sets out the answers.

Ordering

- A company should only order goods and services that are authorised by appropriate personnel and are for the company's benefit (**risk** – the company pays for unnecessary or personal goods).

- A company should only order from authorised suppliers (**risk** – other suppliers may not supply quality goods or may be too expensive).

Receipt of goods and invoices

- A company should ensure that goods and services received are used for the organisation's purposes (**risk** – the company may pay for goods/services for personal use).

- A company should only accept goods that have been ordered (and appropriately authorised) (**risk** – as above).

- A company should record all goods and services received (**risk** – the company fails to pay for goods/services and loses suppliers).

- A company should ensure it claims all credits due to it (**risk** – company pays for poor quality goods).

- A company should not acknowledge liability for goods it has not recorded (**risk** – company pays for goods it has not received).

Accounting

- A company should only make authorised payments for goods that have been received (**risk** – as above).

- A company should record expenditure accurately in the accounting records (**risks** – financial statements are misstated, and the company does not pay for genuine liabilities).

- A company should record credit notes received correctly in the accounting records (**risks** – financial statements are misstated, and the company pays for items unnecessarily).

- A company should record liabilities in the correct purchase ledger accounts (**risk** – company pays the wrong supplier).

- A company should record liabilities in the correct period (**risk** – financial statements are misstated by recording purchase but not inventory or recording inventory, but not the associated liability).

Payments

- A company should only make payments to the correct recipients and for the correct amounts which are authorised (**risk** – company pays the wrong supplier).

- A company should only pay for liabilities once (**risk** – the company pays more than once and the supplier does not correct the mistake).

Task 11

For each of the objectives given in bullet points above, can you think of a control procedure which will help achieve the objective? When you have thought it through, read the next section, which gives you some examples of controls.

Controls in the purchases system

I'll list some examples of control procedures in the purchases system relating to the objectives I outlined above, but before I do, I want to emphasise the importance of segregation of duties in a purchases system.

Task 12

Which stages of the purchases system do you feel ought to be dealt with by different staff members, and why? Read through the following text to see the answer.

The key areas of concern are:

A person could order and pay for personal goods through the company, and this is easier if the person who writes out the cheques also signs the cheques, so these two roles should be separated, as should the roles of ordering and payment.

Other key control procedures are as follows:

Ordering

- A company should have a central policy for choosing suppliers
- Orders should be authorised only when the need for the items has been justified (on a purchase requisition for example)
- Orders should only be prepared when purchase requisitions are received from departments
- Orders should be authorised
- Orders should be pre-numbered and blank order forms should be safeguarded
- Orders not yet received should be reviewed
- Supplier terms should be monitored and advantage taken of discounts offered

Goods and invoices received

- Goods received should be examined for quality and quantity
- Goods received should be recorded on pre-numbered goods received notes
- Goods received notes should be compared with purchase orders
- Supplier invoices should be checked to orders and goods received notes
- Supplier invoices should be referenced (numerical order and supplier reference)
- Supplier invoices should be checked for prices, quantities, calculations
- Goods returned should be recorded on pre-numbered goods returned notes
- There should be procedures for obtaining credit notes from suppliers

Accounting

- Purchases and purchase returns should be promptly recorded in daybooks and ledgers
- The purchase ledger should be regularly maintained
- Supplier statements should be compared with the purchase ledger
- Payments should be authorised and only made if goods have been received
- The purchase ledger control account should be reconciled to the list of balances
- Goods received but not yet invoiced at the year-end should be accrued separately

Payments

- Cheques should be requisitioned and requests evidenced with supporting documentation
- Cheque payments should be authorised by someone other than a signatory
- There should be limitations on the payment amount individual staff members can sign for
- Blank cheques should never be signed
- Signed cheques should be despatched promptly
- Paid cheques should be collected from the bank (ie after the supplier has banked them, the company can get them back as proof)
- Payments should be recorded promptly in the cash book and ledger
- Cash payments should be limited and authorised

Task 13

What are the objectives of the following controls?

- The necessity for orders should be evidenced
- Supplier invoices should be referenced
- Supplier statements should be compared with the purchase ledger
- Blank cheques should never be signed

You should also review the list of all the controls given above and ensure that you understand what the objectives of the controls are.

PAYROLL SYSTEMS

Control objectives in the payroll system

Task 14

Think for a moment about what the aims of an internal control system over payroll are, and what risks it is aiming to mitigate. In doing so, you may find it helpful to think through the stages of paying wages and salaries. When you have thought it through, read the text below which sets out the answers.

Setting pay

- A company should only pay employees for work they have done (**risk** – the company overpays).

- A company should pay employees the correct gross pay, which has previously been authorised (**risk** – as above).

Recording wages and salaries

- A company should record gross pay, net pay, and relevant deductions correctly on the payroll (**risks** – company may make incorrect payments to staff/tax offices and financial statements may be misstated).

- A company should record payments made in the bank and cash records and general ledger (**risk** – financial statements may be misstated).

- A company should comply with the requirements of the Data Protection Act 1998 (**risk** – the company could make unauthorised disclosures of employee information).

Paying wages and salaries

- A company should pay the correct employees (**risks** – angry, unpaid workforce and/or the company overpays – the wrong people).

Deductions

- A company should ensure all deductions have been properly calculated and authorised (**risks** – breaking the law, calculating staff pensions incorrectly leading to staff displeasure).

- A company should ensure they pay the correct amounts to taxation authorities (**risk** – breaking the law and incurring fines).

Task 15

For each of the objectives given in bullet points above, can you think of a control procedure which will help achieve the objective? When you have thought it through, read the next section, which gives you some examples of controls.

Controls in the payroll system

I'll list some examples of control procedures in the payroll system relating to the objectives outlined above, but before I do, I want to emphasise the importance of segregation of duties in a payroll system.

Task 16

Which stages of the payroll system do you feel ought to be dealt with by different staff members, and why? Read through the following text to see the answer.

The danger is that a person could authorise an inappropriate salary for himself, or enter himself on the payroll twice at an appropriate salary. Hence the payroll should be authorised by someone other than the person preparing it. When wages are paid in cash, the danger is that a staff member could steal pay packets, so cash payments should be made by two people.

Other key control activities are as follows:

Setting pay

- Personnel records should be kept and wages and salaries checked to details held in them

- Personnel files should be kept locked up

- Engaging employees, setting rates of pay, changing rates of pay, overtime, non-statutory deductions from pay and advances of pay should all be authorised and recorded

- Changes in personnel and pay rates should be recorded

- Hours worked should be recorded, time should be clocked

- Hours worked should be reviewed

- Payroll should be reviewed against budget

Recording payroll

- Payroll should be prepared, checked and approved before payment

Paying wages and salaries

- Wage cheques for cash payments should be authorised
- Cash should be kept securely
- Identity of staff should be verified before payment
- Distributions of cash wages should be recorded
- Bank transfer lists should be prepared and authorised
- Bank transfer lists should be compared to the payroll

Deductions from pay

- Separate employees' records should be maintained

- Total pay and deductions should be reconciled month-on-month

- Costs of pay should be compared to budgets

- Gross pay and total tax deducted should be checked to returns to the tax authorities

Task 17

What are the objectives of the following controls?

- Changes in personnel should be recorded
- A payroll should be prepared
- Wage cheques for cash payments should be authorised
- Costs of pay should be compared to budgets

You should also review the list of all the controls given above and ensure that you understand what the objectives of the controls are.

NON-CURRENT ASSET SYSTEMS

Control objectives in the non-current asset system

Task 18

Think for a moment about what the aims of an internal control system over non-current assets are, and what risks it is aiming to mitigate. In doing so, you might find it helpful to think through the stages of owning assets. When you have thought it through, read the text below which sets out the answers.

Buying assets

- Non-current asset additions are authorised (**risks** – the company buys assets it does not need and/or at an inappropriate price)

Storing and using assets

- Non-current assets are kept securely (**risk** – the assets are stolen).

- Non-current assets are maintained properly (**risk** – the assets are not fit for use in the business when required).

Selling assets

- Non-current asset disposals are authorised (**risks** – the company sells assets it needs to operate and/or at an inappropriate price).

Recording assets

- Non-current assets are properly accounted for and recorded (**risk** – company misstates non-current assets in the financial statements).

- Depreciation rates are reasonable (**risk** – assets are valued wrongly and financial statements are misstated).

- Proceeds from disposal of non-current assets are recorded (**risks**: proceeds may be stolen or omitted from financial statements, profit or loss on sale of assets may be misstated in financial statements).

Task 19

For each of the objectives given in bullet points above, can you think of a control procedure which will help achieve the objective? When you have thought it through, read the next section, which gives you some examples of controls.

Controls in the non-current asset system

I'll list some examples of control procedures in the non-current asset system relating to the objectives outlined above, but before I do, I want to emphasise the importance of segregation of duties in a non-current asset system.

Task 20

Which stages of the non-current asset system do you feel ought to be dealt with by different staff members, and why? Read through the following text to see the answer.

One danger, given that purchasing is involved, is the same as that in the purchases system, namely that a person could authorise the purchase of an asset that is not required for the business and then use it for personal gain. More generally, anyone could use company assets for their own purposes and risk wear or damage to that asset. In addition, assets could be sold to related parties for inappropriate prices in return for backhanders. It is important then, that authorisation of non-current asset purchases, custody of the assets and recording relating to assets is generally carried out by different people.

Other key control activities are as follows:

Buying assets

- Capital expenditure is budgeted for/authorised by a senior official in the company

Storing and using assets

- A non-current asset register is maintained and compared with actual assets and general ledger record of assets

- Non-current assets are inspected regularly to ensure they are maintained/in use/secure

Selling assets

- Non-current asset sales or scrappage is authorised/planned to avoid business interruption

Recording assets

- Depreciation rates are authorised/checked
- Non-current asset register is maintained

Task 21

What are the objectives of the following control procedures?

- Capital expenditure is authorised
- Non-current assets are inspected regularly
- Asset scrappage is authorised

You should also review the list of all the controls given above and ensure that you understand what the objectives of the controls are.

INVENTORY SYSTEMS

Control objectives in the inventory system

Task 22

Think for a moment about what the aims of an internal control system over inventory are, and what risks it is aiming to mitigate. In doing so, you might find it helpful to think through the stages of inventory use in a business. When you have thought it through, read the text below which sets out the answers.

Recording of inventory

- Inventory movements authorised and recorded (**risk** – inventory might be stolen)

- Inventory records only include items that belong to the company or that exist at all (**risk** – inventory may be overstated in the financial statements)

- Inventory quantities have been recorded correctly (**risks** – the company may have insufficient to operate efficiently and inventory may be misstated in the financial statements)

- Inventory is not recorded as an asset once a sale has been made or before a purchase is recognised (**risk** – the financial statements may be misstated)

Protection of inventory

- Inventory is protected from loss/damage (**risk** – goods might be stolen, or be unusable/unsaleable)

Valuation of inventory

- Inventory is valued correctly (**risk** – inventory may be misstated in the financial statements)

- Slow-moving, obsolete and damaged inventory is noted (**risk** – inventory may be overstated in the financial statements)

Inventory levels

- Levels of inventory held are reasonable (**risk** – the company may not have sufficient inventory to function efficiently)

Task 23

For each of the objectives given in bullet points above, can you think of a control procedure which will help achieve the objective? When you have thought it through, read the next section, which gives you some examples of controls.

Controls in the inventory system

Recording of inventory

- Segregation of duties between custody of inventory and recording
- Checking and recording goods inwards
- Issues of inventory supported by appropriate documentation
- Maintaining inventory records

Protection of inventory

- Restriction of access to stores
- Controls on stores environment (temperature/damp etc)
- Regular inventory counts by independent people
- Reconciliation of inventory count to book records

Valuation of inventory

- Calculation of inventory value and checking of calculation
- Regular review of inventory condition
- Accounting for scrap and waste

Inventory levels

- Maximum and minimum inventory levels set
- Reorder limits set

Task 24

What are the objectives of the following control procedures?

- Restriction of access to stores
- Regular inventory counts
- Review of condition of inventory
- Reorder limits set

You should also review the list of all the controls given above and ensure that you understand what the objectives of the controls are.

CHAPTER OVERVIEW

- Companies set up systems of internal control in order to achieve company objectives and mitigate risks

- An internal control system comprises:

    - Control environment
    - Entity's risk assessment process
    - Information system
    - Control activities
    - Monitoring of controls

- Key objectives in the sales system:

    - Selling to good credit risks
    - Fulfilling orders correctly
    - Invoicing despatched goods
    - Recording sales
    - Identifying irrecoverable receivables
    - Recording payments
    - Banking payments

- Key objectives in the purchases system:

    - Only ordering goods for business
    - Ordering goods at right price
    - Recording goods received
    - Recognising genuine liabilities
    - Recording expenditure properly
    - Making correct payments

- Key objectives in the payroll system:

    - Paying employees for work done
    - Paying correct employees correctly
    - Recording wages and salaries paid
    - Calculating/paying deductions correctly

- Key objectives in the non-current assets system:

    - Purchasing the right assets at the right price
    - Maintaining assets for use
    - Disposing of assets properly
    - Valuing assets appropriately

- Key objectives in the inventory system:

    - Protection of inventory
    - Maintaining appropriate inventory levels

Keywords

Internal control – the process designed, implemented and maintained by those charged with governance (the directors), management, and other personnel to provide reasonable assurance about the achievement of the entity's objectives with regard to the reliability of financial reporting, effectiveness and efficiency of operations and compliance with applicable laws and regulations

Business risk – the risk that the company will not meet its objectives

Control environment – the attitudes, awareness and actions of management and those charged with governance about internal control and its importance

Information system – consists of infrastructure (physical and hardware components), software, people, procedures and data

Control activities – are the policies and procedures that help ensure that management directives are carried out

Application controls – are controls relating to the transactions and standing data relevant to each computer-based accounting system and are specific to each such application

General IT controls – are controls other than application controls relating to the computer environment

Monitoring of controls – a process to assess the quality of internal control performance over time

TEST YOUR LEARNING

Test 1 Complete the following statement describing an internal control system, by filling in the gaps using the items in the pick list below.

Internal control is the process .... , implemented and .... by

....

... , ... and other personnel to provide .... about the achievement of the entity's .... with regard to the reliability of .... , effectiveness and efficiency of .... and compliance with applicable laws and regulations

Pick list

Those charged with governance

Operations

Financial reporting

Management

Designed

Maintained

Reasonable assurance

Objectives

Test 2 Accounting systems have control objectives and control procedures to mitigate the risk that the control objective is not met.

For each of the following select whether they are a control objective, risk, or control procedure.

	Options
A company should only pay for work done by employees.	Control objective Risk Control procedure
Company vehicles are used by employees for their own purposes.	Control objective Risk Control procedure
Part C39t99, in regular use in the business, is reordered when inventory levels fall below 200.	Control objective Risk Control procedure

Test 3 Select whether the following statements in respect of a company's control environment are True or False.

	Options
The directors can ensure a good control environment by implementing controls themselves and never bypassing them.	True / False
The directors should not assign authority for control areas to members of staff.	True / False
A good control environment always leads to a good system of control overall.	True / False

Test 4 Which one of the following statements concerning small and large companies is the least true?

Control activities will be similar in all sizes of company over core activities ☐

A large company is likely to have a more formal control system than a small company ☐

A small company is likely to have a less complex information system than a big company ☐

A large company is more likely to have a good control environment than a small company ☐

Test 5 Which one of the following best describes who undertakes the role of monitoring controls at a company?

A   Controls are always monitored by an internal audit function, as this is the purpose of their existence ☐

B   Controls are monitored by the directors of a company ☐

C   Controls are monitored by the people who operate them, as they are in the best position to assess whether the objectives of the controls are being met ☐

D   Who monitors controls depends on the size of the company and its personnel: it may be an internal audit function, but it could also be the directors, or department heads ☐

Test 6 Set out four key objectives in a sales system.

Test 7 For each control objective you identified in question 6, set out examples of control procedures.

Test 8 Look back to the description of the information system for purchases at HEC given earlier in the chapter. Set out any control procedures existing in the system and suggest others.

Test 9 The personnel director at Metal Extrusions Midlands Limited (MEM) has contacted the audit firm and said that she wants to overhaul the internal control system over wages and salaries at MEM. All members of staff (waged and salaried) are paid by bank transfer. Waged staff members are paid weekly and salaried staff members are paid monthly. At present, the payroll is prepared and authorised by the personnel director, who has sole access to employee records. The bank transfer is authorised by the personnel director but enacted by the cashier.

Task

Set out the control objectives that the personnel director of MEM should consider when putting together a new control system for wages and salaries.

Test 10 Listed below are two control procedures that the directors have put into action at MEM as a result of your recommendations.

For each internal control procedure, use the pick list below to match the procedure with the control objective.

Internal control procedure	Control objective
The payroll should be reconciled to other records, such as the cash payment for net pay per the bank.	
The payroll should be authorised by someone other than the personnel director	

Pick list

- Gross pay, net pay and deductions should be correctly recorded on payroll

- Employees should only be paid for work done

- Gross pay should be calculated correctly and authorised

- Wages and salaries paid should be recorded properly in bank records

Test 11 An entity uses internal control procedures in order to mitigate the risk to which it is exposed. Listed below are two internal control procedures which are applicable to an entity's non-current assets system.

For each internal control procedure, use the pick list below to match the procedure with the risk mitigated.

Internal control procedure	Risk mitigated
Non-current assets are inspected regularly	
Capital expenditure is approved by the purchasing director on behalf of the board	

Pick list

- Assets are not maintained properly for use in the business
- Assets are sold when they are needed for use in the business
- Assets are bought from inappropriate suppliers at inflated cost
- Assets are depreciated incorrectly

Test 12 An entity uses internal control procedures in order to mitigate the risk to which it is exposed. Listed below are two internal control procedures which are applicable to an entity's inventory system.

For each internal control procedure, use the pick list below to match the procedure with the risk mitigated.

Internal control procedure	Risk mitigated
Inventory store is kept locked	
Goods inwards are checked for quality	

Pick list

- Damaged inventory is valued in the financial statements
- Inventory is counted in the financial statements without corresponding creditor
- The company fails to order required goods
- Inventory is stolen

chapter 4:
AUDITING SYSTEMS

─────── **chapter coverage** 📖 ───────

In this chapter I will show you what parts of a company's internal control systems auditors are interested in and the work that they carry out on them. I am booked to do some interim audit work on controls at Metal Extrusions Midlands Limited, so you can come along and do that with me. The topics covered are:

✍ Ascertaining systems

✍ Confirming systems

✍ Evaluating systems

✍ Testing controls

✍ Reporting on systems

ASCERTAINING SYSTEMS

Auditors must satisfy themselves that the systems of a company are capable of producing financial statements.

They will also consider the risk of the system not preventing or not detecting and correcting errors. If the system does not prevent or detect errors, then those errors will carry through to the financial statements. I'll tell you more about risk in auditing in the next chapter, so don't worry about it too much here. But you should know at this stage that the auditors' evaluation of the control system will affect the type of testing that the auditors carry out as part of their audit.

Basically, if the auditors believe that controls operate well, they will test them, and that will enable them to reduce the amount of detailed testing they carry out on other areas on the audit (the audit tests that we look at in Chapters 7 to 9).

In order to evaluate and test the system, the auditors need first to ascertain it, meaning that they need to get to know it. This is achieved by:

- Making enquiries of staff (enquiry)
- Watching the system in operation (observation)

They will make SYSTEMS NOTES, a record of how the internal control system operates.

As a company's system will often not change radically from year-to-year, systems notes will often be completed in the year the audit firm first audits the client and then **updated annually** for any changes.

We look at a number of ways here in which these systems notes can be updated.

Narrative notes

NARRATIVE NOTES are a narrative record of how the system works. Their purpose is to describe and explain the system.

They are the most straightforward of the types of systems notes, but, particularly if they are handwritten, can be awkward to update efficiently if the system changes. This problem is not so great if the notes are computerised.

The notes need to answer questions such as:

- Who does what?
- What documents do they use in doing it?
- Where do documents start from and where are they going?
- Where are documents retained and in what sequence?
- What books are kept and where?

Narrative notes can in fact be kept to support flowcharts (which we study next), which illustrate the answers to the above questions in more a more pictorial format.

Flowcharts

FLOWCHARTS are a picture of the system and how it operates. Here is a basic example of a flowchart.

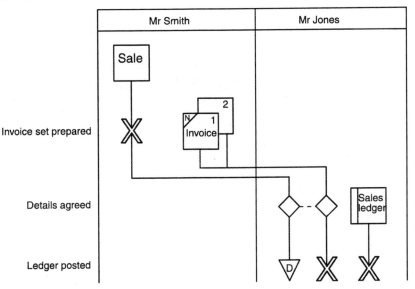

In practice, even in small companies, a flowchart is likely to grow more complex than this simple example.

Advantages of flowcharts

  (a) After a little experience they can be prepared quickly

  (b) As the information is presented in a standard form, they are fairly easy to follow and to review

  (c) They generally ensure that the system is recorded in its entirety, as all document flows have to be traced from beginning to end. Any 'loose ends' will be apparent from a quick examination

  (d) They eliminate the need for extensive narrative and can be of considerable help in highlighting the salient points of control and any deficiencies in the system

On the other hand, flowcharts do have some *disadvantages.*

  (a) They are only really suitable for describing standard systems. Procedures for dealing with unusual transactions will normally have to be recorded using narrative notes

  (b) They are useful for recording the flow of documents, but once the records or the assets to which they relate have become static they can no longer be used for describing the controls (for example, over non-current assets)

  (c) Major amendment is difficult without redrawing

Internal control questionnaires (ICQ) and checklists

An INTERNAL CONTROL QUESTIONNAIRE is a list of questions designed to find out if suitable controls are present. They are designed so that a 'yes' answer indicates that a suitable control is present and a 'no' answer indicates that a suitable control is not present.

HOW IT WORKS

Here is an example internal control questionnaire I filled in at HEC last year.

Internal control questionnaire: HEC Wages system		
Question	Y/N	Comment
Are personnel records kept for each member of staff containing details of wage rates?	Yes	
Does a senior member of staff authorise new employees and changes in rates of pay?	Yes	Peter or Rosemary approve any changes
Are any changes in pay rates recorded in the personnel records?	Yes	Updated by Peter or Rosemary
Are hours worked recorded on timesheets?	No	Peter and Rosemary keep informal watch on hours worked
Are hours worked reviewed?	Yes	See above
Are wages reviewed against budget?	No	Budget preparation is very informal – see general comments on page x.
Is a payroll prepared and approved before payment?	Yes	Prepared by accountant monthly and approved by Rosemary before payment
Are total pay and deductions reconciled month-on-month?	Yes	Done by accountant
Are bank transfer lists prepared and authorised?	Yes	Rosemary prepares instructions for the bank, which Peter approves

Task 1

Draft an internal control questionnaire for the purchases system at MEM.

Checklists

Checklists are very similar in principle to internal control questionnaires. They are simply checklists of controls that an auditor would expect to be in place at a client. An auditor would ascertain whether these suitable controls were in place by asking the client staff.

Internal control questionnaires and checklists are in general terms more standardised than narrative notes or flowcharts which are created specifically for the client's system. The auditor must not ignore genuine controls in the client's system because they are not covered by the standardised list of questions. Often a questionnaire will be used in conjunction with narrative notes, or in order to facilitate creating narrative notes.

CONFIRMING SYSTEMS

Once the auditor has ascertained the system, he should confirm that the system operates as he has been told it will.

Task 2

How might an auditor confirm that the system operates as he has been told?

The best way of confirming the system is to carry out a walk-through test. A WALK-THROUGH TEST is when the auditors select a transaction and trace it through the system to see the evidence of the control procedures they have been told about. In other words, they will inspect the order, the invoice, the goods note and the ledger records.

An auditor is likely to carry out a walk-through test on a sale, a purchase and a wages transaction.

Walking through the system provides better evidence for the auditor than simply observing how it works, because the staff might be biased when the auditor is watching them and operate control procedures they usually don't bother with in normal circumstances.

EVALUATING SYSTEMS

Once the auditors have ascertained and confirmed the system, they will evaluate it to assess whether the systems are capable of producing financial statements that are free from errors.

The auditors will use their expertise and knowledge to assess whether systems appear to be good and are capable of achieving their objectives. They will also evaluate whether they appear to work in practice.

In other words, they will evaluate two matters:

- The **design** of the system
- The **operation** of the system

Once the auditors have evaluated the system, they will decide on audit approach.

If the auditors believe that controls are effective, they will test them. This means that they will go on to take what is called a **combined approach** to the audit, where they test both controls and balances and transactions in the financial statements.

If the auditors believe that controls are not effective, they will not test controls, but will take what is called a **substantive approach** to the audit. This involves only testing balances and transactions. Such tests are carried out in more detail than they would under the combined approach.

If the auditors believe that controls are substantially ineffective, they may have to determine whether they are capable of creating financial statements at all. If they believe that they are not, the auditors will not be able to give an opinion on the financial statements, and will have to report to members that the directors have not kept adequate records (the legal requirement we discussed in Chapter 1).

TESTING CONTROLS

TESTS OF CONTROLS are tests to obtain evidence about the effective operation of the accounting and internal control systems.

Auditors will ask:

- Were controls applied?
- Who applied them?
- Were they applied correctly?

The tests they apply to find answers to these questions might include:

- Asking client staff (this type of test is called **enquiry**) (this type of test alone is not sufficient and should be used together with other tests)

- Looking at documents to see whether controls took place (this type of test is called **inspection**)

- Discovering management opinion by looking at minutes of management meetings, for example (also **inspection**)

- Redoing control procedures, to ensure they were done properly, for example, reconciliations (this type of test is called **reperformance**)

- Testing controls on computerised applications (this type of test may involve using a **CAAT** – see below)

- Looking at client staff operating the system (this type of test is called **observation**)

When are tests of control carried out?

It is vital that auditors test controls over the whole of the period being audited, not just at one point in the year, as various factors could affect the operation of controls at different times.

Now that we have talked about tests of controls in general terms, let's look at some examples relating to the purchases cycle.

Purchases system

Ordering

A key objective is that orders are for authorised goods or services. Tests of controls are as follows.

- Check that all **invoices** are **supported** by authorised **purchase invoices** and **purchase orders**

Receipt of goods and services

All goods and services received should be recorded and liabilities duly recognised. Tests of controls include the following.

- Check invoices for goods, raw materials are:
    - Supported by goods received notes and inspection notes
    - Entered in inventory records
    - Priced correctly by checking to quotations, price lists to ensure the price is accurate
    - Properly referenced with a number and supplier code
    - Correctly coded by type of expenditure
- **Trace entry in record of goods returned** and see credit note duly received from the supplier, for invoices not passed due to defects or discrepancy
- For invoices of all types:
    - Check calculations and additions
    - Check entries in purchase day book and verify that they are correctly analysed
    - Check posting to purchase ledger
- For credit notes:
    - **Verify** the **correctness** of credit received with correspondence
    - **Check entries** in **inventory records**
    - **Check entries** in **record of returns**
    - **Check entries** in **purchase day book** and verify that they are correctly analysed
    - **Check postings** to **purchase ledger**

- Check for **returns** that **credit notes** are duly **received** from the suppliers

- Test **numerical sequence** and enquire into missing numbers of:
    - Purchase requisitions
    - Purchase orders
    - Goods received notes
    - Goods returned notes
    - Suppliers' invoices

- **Obtain explanations** for **items** which have been **outstanding** for a long time:
    - Unmatched purchase requisitions
    - Purchase orders
    - Goods received notes (if invoices not received)
    - Unprocessed invoices

Recording of expenditure

Objectives include ensuring all expenditure is properly recorded. Tests of controls include the following.

Purchase day book

- Verify that invoices and credit notes recorded in the purchase day book are:
    - **Initialled** for prices, calculations and extensions
    - **Cross-referenced** to purchase orders, goods received notes
    - **Authorised** for payment
- **Check additions**
- **Check postings** to general ledger accounts and control account
- **Check postings** of entries to purchase ledger

Purchase ledger

- For a sample of accounts recorded in the purchase ledger:
    - **Test check entries** back into books of prime entry
    - **Test check additions** and **balances** forward
    - **Note** and **enquire** into all contra entries

- Confirm **control account balancing** has been regularly carried out during the year

- **Examine control account** for unusual entries

Cash payments

Auditors will be concerned with whether **payments** have been **authorised** and are to the **correct payee**.

Tests of controls

- For a sample of payments in the cash book:

    - **Compare** with paid cheques to ensure payee agrees

    - **Check** that **cheques** are **signed** by the **persons authorised** to do so within their authority limits

    - **Check** to **suppliers' invoices** for goods and services. Verify that supporting documents are signed as having been **checked** and **passed for payment** and have been stamped 'paid'

    - **Check** supplier details and amounts to **suppliers' statements**

    - **Check** details to **other documentary evidence**, as appropriate (agreements, authorised expense vouchers, wages/salaries records, petty cash books etc)

Task 3

The narrative notes for the sales system at MEM Ltd are given below.

'Sales orders are taken by the sales department, usually by phone. The sales department consists of the sales director, Ted Bishop and his assistant, Sandra Dales. When they take an order from an existing customer, they check that the customer does not have outstanding orders which exceed the credit limit on the account. They then record the order on a three-part, pre-numbered sales order document. Only Ted is allowed to authorise individual sales orders in excess of £20,000.

When a new customer makes an order, Sandra passes the query to Ted, who carries out a credit check before the order is accepted and then sets a credit limit based on that check. Only then is the order accepted and processed.

One copy of the sales order is filed in the client file in the sales department, and two are sent to the production department to start work on the order. The production controller, Ben Swales, determines when the order can be fulfilled by, which is written on the two copies of the sales order. One is then sent to the customer and the other is retained in the 'orders pending' file in Ben's office until the order has been completed.

When the order is ready to be despatched, Ben checks the date, and if the order has been completed early, telephones the customer to ensure it is okay to despatch the order. Before goods are despatched, they are checked for quality and quantity against the order by Ian Mellor, the factory foreman. He then completes a two-part, pre-numbered goods despatch note. One copy is sent out to the customer with the goods, the other, stamped 'despatched' is matched with the production copy of the sales order and sent to the accounts department. Goods are not despatched after 3pm.

At 3.30pm, in the accounts department, Tessa Goodyear raises the invoices based on the goods despatch notes she has been sent by the production department. The invoices are created on the computer by her entering the appropriate details. The computer gives her a sequential number for each invoice. Prices are automatically inserted on the invoice from the price list when she inputs the inventory number. If a special price has been negotiated, this will be stated on the sales order attached to the goods despatch note, and she will have to manually override the price given by the computer. She prints off the invoices and checks that they are calculated correctly. One copy of the invoice is matched with the order and GDN and filed, numerically, in the accounts department. The other copy is sent out. The computer automatically updates a sales daybook and the sales ledger for the invoiced sales. Sometimes, not all the invoices are completed until the next morning. The invoices are always sent out in one batch.

The accounts department receive the post at 10am, when it has been sorted by the managing director's secretary. The post is opened by Tessa Goodyear and Paula Taylor, the cashier, who makes a list of all the sales ledger receipts. The cheques are placed in the safe until they are banked in the afternoon, by Paula Taylor. Paula then enters the receipts in the cashbook on the computer. The cashbook programme automatically updates the sales ledger.

The financial controller, Marie Edgehill, reconciles the sales ledger control account on a monthly basis.

Every Monday, Tessa Goodyear prints an aged debt report off the sales ledger and reviews it for potentially irrecoverable receivables. She then takes appropriate action, which is usually to highlight potential problems to Marie, or to telephone customers to ask when they are going to be able to pay. In rare circumstances, MEM uses a debt collection service to enforce very late debts.'

Task 1

Identify five control procedures operating in this system.

Task 2

Outline a test of control that could be conducted on each control identified.

Task 4

Which of the following tests confirms that the company has an effective control to purchase appropriate non-current assets?

A   Inspect asset register to ensure new assets have been included.

B   Inspect purchase order and ensure matched with purchase invoice.

C   Check sales invoices for proceeds relating to sale of assets.

D   Review purchase order for evidence of authorisation.

Computer-assisted audit techniques (CAATs)

COMPUTER-ASSISTED AUDIT TECHNIQUES are audit techniques carried out by use of the computer by the auditor.

CAATs can be intrusive and should only be used with client permission. Clearly, the client will not want the auditors' software to cause problems in his own computer systems.

Two key types of CAAT are audit software and test data.

Audit software is software which can check data on computer systems by interrogating it or comparing versions of programmes. It could therefore be used to check the reliability of balances by performing comparisons for the auditor to analyse (analytical procedures) or to select a sample for the auditor to carry out manual checks on.

Test data is a way of checking computer processing, by inputting real data into the system and ensuring that it is processed correctly, or not processed. If the data is deliberately false it should be incapable of being processed. This is a way that an auditor can test controls, particularly in a highly computerised system.

When a system is highly computerised, the auditor may find using CAATs extremely beneficial in terms of time and efficiency. It is a reasonable general rule to say CAATs are more likely to be used for large clients, particularly if they have complex computerised systems.

Task 5

Two types of computer-assisted audit techniques (CAAT) are test data and audit software.

For each of the procedures listed below, select the type of CAAT which would be used to perform that procedure.

	Options
Extraction of all receivables balances older than 120 days to perform irrecoverable receivable work.	Audit software Test data
Input of purchase invoices with false customer numbers to ensure that the system rejects the invoices.	Audit software Test data
Comparison of suppliers on ledger with previous years to discover any new or missing suppliers.	Audit software Test data

REPORTING ON SYSTEMS

Auditors are required by auditing standards to make certain communications with those charged with governance and management in an organisation being audited.

THOSE CHARGED WITH GOVERNANCE are the persons responsible for directing the company under law. In the UK, these are the directors of the company.

Under ISA 265 *Communicating Deficiencies in Internal Control to Those Charged With Governance and Management*, auditors are required to communicate any significant deficiencies in the accounting and control systems identified during the audit. A DEFICIENCY IN INTERNAL CONTROL is when a control is designed, implemented or operated in such a way that it is unable to prevent, or detect and correct, misstatements in the financial statements on a timely basis, or a necessary control is missing.

Deficiencies become significant when the auditor judges that they should be communicated to those charged with governance, perhaps because their potential effect is so great, or because there are so many of them.

The communication must be made **in writing**. Significant deficiencies should also be communicated with management in writing, and other deficiencies should be discussed with management if the auditors judge it necessary.

When the auditors communicate the deficiencies, they must set out each weakness (deficiency) and outline the implications for the company. They would usually 'add value' by suggesting an improvement that could be made to prevent the deficiency. The report issued should explain that the deficiencies have been discovered during audit work, and that it is not a comprehensive review of the systems.

HOW IT WORKS

Here are some extracts from the report on control deficiencies issued after the audit of HEC last year. They focus on deficiencies in the sales system.

Mason & Co
1 High Street
Oxtown, O2 4ED

The board of directors
The Heavenly Eating Company Ltd
8 High Street
Smallville

28 April 20X8

Members of the board,

Financial statements for the year ended 31 December 20X7

In accordance with our normal practice we set out in this letter certain matters which arose as a result of our review of the accounting systems and procedures operated by your company during our recent audit.

We would point out that the matters dealt with in this letter came to our notice during the conduct of our normal audit procedures which are designed primarily for the purpose of expressing our opinion on the financial statements of your company. In consequence, our work did not encompass a detailed review of all aspects of the system and cannot be relied on necessarily to disclose defalcations or other irregularities or to include all possible improvements in internal control.

1   Sales: despatch

Present system. Despatches of sales are not cross-checked to the original order noted in the sales order book.

Implications. Incorrect deliveries could be sent out to customers resulting in potential loss to HEC (if the goods are perishable or customised and cannot be resold) with potential loss of customer goodwill.

Recommendation. Before an order is despatched, it should be checked against the order book to ensure that it meets the requirements of the order as to goods and quantity. A quality check should also be carried out at this stage. We recommend that this check be evidenced by the checker writing the reference of the despatch document on the sales order book and initialling to show that the check was made.

2   *Sales ledger: credit control*

Present system. At present, the sales ledger is extracted monthly by the company accountant.

Implications. This has implications for efficient credit control, as some transactions may have occurred a month before the ledger is even written-up and a receipt might be due immediately subsequent to the date the ledger is written-up. However, if this receipt is not forthcoming, it could be overdue before the ledger is written up again, and no action may have been taken to chase that late payment as a result of the timing of the sales ledger being updated.

Recommendation. The sales ledger should be written-up on a more frequent basis. If possible, this should be carried out weekly. However, a fortnightly basis would also improve the situation. If it is not practical for the company to get the sales ledger written-up more than monthly, HEC should start a system of checking for slow paying debts by comparing receipts to entries in the sales day book.

3   *Sales system: segregation of duties*

Present system. At present, Peter Tyme is in charge of recording all elements of a sales transaction (order, despatch, invoice and payment), although the accountant extracts the information into the ledgers on a monthly basis

Implications. Peter could make errors in processing that would not necessarily be discovered by the accountant in extracting the ledger and even if they were discovered, it might not be until some time after the error had been made.

In addition, such a lack of segregation of duties makes it far easier to commit a fraud on the company in respect of sales. Although Peter is a part-owner and might be considered to be unlikely to commit a fraud on his company, it would be better practice to ensure that more segregation was introduced.

Recommendation. As a minimum, a different member of staff should be involved in recording sales receipts.

Our comments have been discussed with your sales director and these matters will be considered by us again during future audits. We look forward to receiving your comments on the points made. Should you require any further information or explanations do not hesitate to contact us.

This letter has been produced for the sole use of your company. It must not be disclosed to a third party, or quoted or referred to, without our written consent. No responsibility is assumed by us to any other person.

We should like to take this opportunity of thanking your staff for their co-operation and assistance during the course of our audit.

Yours faithfully

Mason & Co

Clearly, a key skill in reporting control deficiencies to those charged with governance and management is being able to identify control deficiencies in the first place, and being able to suggest improvements in the system.

Task 6

Using the information given about MEM's system in Task 3, using the options list below, state whether the following are strengths or deficiencies of MEM's system or potentially both.

	Options
Only Ted Bishop is allowed to authorise new customers and orders over £20,000	Strength Deficiency Potentially both
Orders are recorded on pre-numbered sales orders	Strength Deficiency Potentially both
Goods are sometimes ready for despatch early	Strength Deficiency Potentially both
It is necessary for Tessa to manually override the price system on the computer if a special price has been negotiated	Strength Deficiency Potentially both

Task 7

Look back to the description of the information system for purchases at HEC given on page 41 in Chapter 3.

Task

Identify any weaknesses in the system and draft the relevant segments of a report on internal control deficiencies relating to those deficiencies (weakness, implication, recommendation). Note you do not have to draft any of the other elements of the report.

CHAPTER OVERVIEW

- Auditors must ascertain a company's systems

- They do this by a combination of enquiry and observation of client staff

- They then record the system in systems notes, which may be:

    - Narrative notes
    - Flowcharts
    - Internal control questionnaire
    - Checklist

- Once they have ascertained the system, auditors carry out walk-through tests

- Once they have confirmed the system, auditors should evaluate it

- If they feel that the system operates effectively, they test controls. If they feel it does not operate efficiently, they may choose not to

- If the auditors feel that the system appears to be so ineffective it may not be able to produce financial statements, they may have to consider whether they can give an audit opinion at all

- There are various tests that an auditor can carry out on controls, including enquiry, inspection, reperformance and observation

- If the client's system is computerised, the auditor may be able to make use of computer-assisted audit techniques

- Auditors must report any significant deficiencies in control they find to those charged with governance and management, in writing

- Weaknesses are reported in the format of weakness, implication and recommendation

Keywords

Systems notes – a record of how the internal control system operates

Narrative notes – a narrative record of how the system works

Flowcharts – a picture of the system and how it operates

Internal control questionnaire – a list of questions designed to find out if suitable controls are present

Walk-through test – when the auditors select a transaction and trace it through the system to ensure that the system operates as they have been told

Tests of controls – tests to obtain evidence about the effective operation of the accounting and internal control systems

Computer-assisted audit techniques – audit techniques carried out by use of the computer by the auditor

Those charged with governance – are the persons responsible for directing the company under the law

A **deficiency in internal control** – when a control is designed, implemented or operated in such a way that it is unable to prevent, or detect and correct, misstatements in the financial statements on a timely basis, or a necessary control is missing

TEST YOUR LEARNING

Test 1 Complete the following statements on the auditor's work on internal control systems, by filling in the gaps using the items listed in the pick list below.

– Auditors ascertain the client's system by a combination of .... and ....

– Auditors confirm that the system operates as intended by conducting a ....

– If auditors believe that the control system is strong, they will take a .... approach to the audit.

– If auditors believe the control system to be weak, they will take a more .... approach to the audit.

Pick list

Combined

Walkthrough test

Observation

Substantive

Enquiry

Test 2 External auditors use a variety of methods for documenting systems of control, including flowcharts, internal control questionnaires and checklists.

For each of the following descriptions, select whether it represents a flowchart, internal control questionnaire or internal control checklist.

	Options
A series of questions designed to identify controls in a system. A no answer indicates a weakness in controls	Flowchart ICQ Checklist
A graphic rendition of the system, using conventional symbols to represent controls and documents	Flowchart ICQ Checklist

Test 3 When documenting systems, the auditor will use the most appropriate method. Using the options listed below, indicate which is the most appropriate method to achieve the objectives outlined below.

	Options
The systems notes should be easy to follow at a glance and easy to review	Narrative notes Flowchart Questionnaire
The systems notes should be comprehensive and detailed, and, if computerised, easy to update	Narrative notes Flowchart Questionnaire
The systems notes should follow the firm's standard and should be easy for staff to use	Narrative notes Flowchart Questionnaire

Test 4 State whether the following statements are True or False in respect of recording of systems.

	Options
A yes answer to an internal control questionnaire indicates that a control exists	True False
A yes answer to an internal control questionnaire indicates that the auditors can rely on a control in the system for the purposes of their audit	True False

Test 5 State whether the following statements are True or False in respect of the auditors' evaluation of a client's internal control system.

	Options
When an auditor evaluates an internal control system he is concerned with the design of internal controls	True False
When an auditor evaluates an internal control system he is concerned with the operation of internal controls	True False

Test 6 Complete the following statement on computer-assisted audit techniques, by filling in the gaps using the items in the pick list below.

Computer-assisted audit techniques are methods of obtaining .... by using ....

.... is .... that can check .... on computer systems by .... or by comparing versions of ....

.... is a way of checking computer .... by inputting real or false information and observing how the programme deals with it

Pick list

Evidence

Audit software

Programming

Test data

Computers

Software

Data

Interrogating

Programmes

Test 7 Companies set up systems of control to mitigate risks to the business. External auditors may seek to rely on these controls in order to reduce detailed testing.

For each of the following, select whether it is a control objective, a control activity, or a test of control, using the options listed below.

	Options
Observe post opening	Control objective Control activity Test of control
Safeguard blank purchase order forms	Control objective Control activity Test of control
Review numerical sequence of goods received notes	Control objective Control activity Test of control

Test 8 Here is the purchases system at MEM, presented in flowchart form.

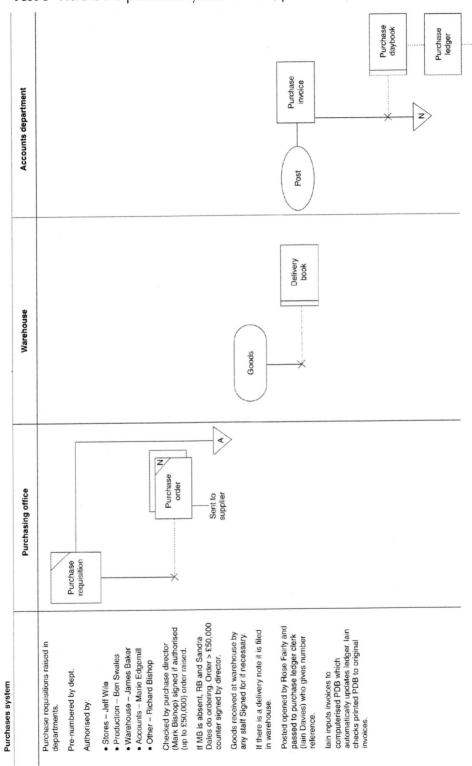

Metal Extrusions Midlands Limited
Purchases system

Purchasing office
Warehouse
Accounts department

Purchase requisitions raised in departments.

Pre-numbered by dept.

Authorised by:

- Stores – Jeff Wile
- Production – Ben Swales
- Warehouse – James Baker
- Accounts – Marie Edgemill
- Other – Richard Bishop

Checked by purchase director (Mark Bishop) signed if authorised (up to £50,000) order raised.

If MB is absent, RB and Sandra Dales do ordering. Order > £50,000 counter signed by director.

Goods received at warehouse by any staff Signed for if necessary.

If there is a delivery note it is filed in warehouse.

Posted opened by Rose Fairly and passed to purchase ledger clerk (Iain Davies) who gives number reference.

Iain inputs invoices to computerised PDB which automatically updates ledger. Iain checks printed PDB to original invoices.

Purchase requisition

Purchase order

Sent to supplier

Goods

Delivery book

Post

Purchase invoice

Purchase daybook

Purchase ledger

Metal Extrusions

Purchasing office	Warehouse	Accounts department

Iain compares statements to ledger and works out differences (usually timing).

Iain produces payment run based on credit terms (automatic by the computer)

Paula prepares cheques

Marie Edgehill authorises and signs
Iain sends cheques to customers

Supplier statement

A

Payment report

Cheques

to supplier

Cash book

Identify any weaknesses in the purchase system at MEM and draft appropriate paragraphs to appear in a report to management concerning those control weaknesses.

Test 9 Here is a completed internal control questionnaire about controls in the wages system at MEM.

Internal control questionnaire: HEC wages system		
Question	Y/N	Comment
Are personnel records kept for each member of staff containing details of wage rates?	Yes	Kept in wages office
Does a senior member of staff authorise new employees and changes in rates of pay?	Yes	Authorised by Richard Bishop or Mark Bishop
Are any changes in pay rates recorded in the personnel records?	Yes	By personnel director, Cathy
Are hours worked recorded on timesheets/clocked?	Yes	Clock system in use
Is overtime approved by a senior member of staff?	Yes	Department heads review clock reports weekly
Are hours worked reviewed?	Yes	"
Are wages reviewed against budget?	No	
Is a payroll prepared and approved before payment?	Yes	Prepared by Cathy, approved by Richard
Are total pay and deductions reconciled month-on-month?	Yes	
Where wages are paid in cash, is the wage cheque authorised?	N/A	
Is cash for wages payment kept securely?	N/A	
Is the identity of staff verified before cash payments are made?	N/A	
Are distributions of cash wages recorded?	N/A	
Are unclaimed wages kept securely?	N/A	
Where wages are paid by bank transfer, are transfer lists prepared and authorised?	Yes	Computer produces from payroll Richard authorises
Are transfer lists compared to the payroll?	Yes	"
Are details of deductions kept on employees' individual files?	Yes	
Are total pay and deductions reconciled month-on-month?	Yes	Computer highlights any discrepancies
Are costs of pay compared to budgets?	No	
Are gross pay and tax deducted per the payroll reconciled to returns made to the tax authorities?	Yes	Returns to tax office drafted from payroll by Cathy

Task 1

Identify any weaknesses in the wages system at MEM and draft appropriate paragraphs to appear in a report to management concerning those control weaknesses.

Task 2

Suggest tests which might be appropriate in determining whether the controls over hours worked operate as indicated in the questionnaire.

Test 10 The following are descriptions of procedures within the sales system of Ruby Limited.

For each procedure, state whether it is a strength or a weakness, using the options detailed below.

	Options
When an order is received Miss Dea, in sales, sends out a three-part pre-numbered despatch note to the inventory department	Strength Weakness
The goods are sent to the despatch team, who send out the goods. They complete the despatch note, one copy is sent with the goods, one copy is matched with the order and filed, the other is sent to the accounts department for invoicing	Strength Weakness
Goods are invoiced by Mrs Soule, who also posts sales receipts to the ledger and manages credit control	Strength Weakness

chapter 5:
ASSESSING RISKS

— chapter coverage 📖 —

Well, you now know how to familiarise yourself with a client's system, and how and why to evaluate it. Understanding controls is just one of the areas of understanding you need before carrying out an audit, so we'd better work through the rest as well. I mentioned the issue of risk when we were talking about company systems. Risk has a central part in an audit, and is not restricted to control risk.

Auditors assess risks including the risk of fraud to discover what to test to gain evidence towards their auditor's opinion. Auditors assess risks, then respond to assessed risk by determining the type of tests and procedures to carry out. We look at responding to assessed risks in Chapters 6 to 9. The topics covered in this chapter are:

✍ Understanding the entity and its environment

✍ Audit risk

✍ Materiality

✍ Assessing audit risk

✍ Significant risks: fraud

UNDERSTANDING THE ENTITY AND ITS ENVIRONMENT

We have already talked at length about the entity's internal control system, which is extremely important to auditors.

The other areas of the entity the auditor needs to understand are:

- Industry, regulatory, and other external factors, including the applicable financial reporting framework

- Nature of the entity, including the entity's selection and application of accounting policies

- Objectives and strategies and the related business risks that may result in a material misstatement of the financial statements

- Measurement and review of the entity's financial performance

I'll talk you through a few issues in each of these areas in turn.

Industry, regulatory and other external factors

Well, what does this mean? It means anything to go with the context in which the company operates, and includes matters such as:

- Competition
- Suppliers and customers
- Technology
- Financial reporting requirements
- Legal context
- Political context
- Environmental context
- General economic conditions

It may be a little difficult to see what some of these mean in practice. But the political context of a company could be important if the company manufactures products that a government is trying to discourage in the nation – for example, tobacco products. The legal context is important if a company is in a highly regulated industry, for example, food provision or childcare. Some of the other factors are more specific to the company itself, for example, the competitors it has and how it deals with them in practice, or the relationship it has with suppliers and customers and its practices to retain old custom and obtain new custom.

Nature of the entity

The nature of the entity obviously relates to internal factors: the way that the company is structured and run, the nature of its products and the relationships between the various stakeholders in the company.

STAKEHOLDERS are people with an interest in the company. That interest might be ownership (shareholders), management (directors), employment (employees), demand-related (customers), economic (suppliers), social (local society) or any other interest an individual or group of individuals might have in the company.

It also relates to how a company is financed (this affects the stakeholders, as any lenders will also become stakeholders) and whether the company has related companies or joint ventures.

Objectives and strategies and related business risks

This is the company's response to the previous two issues, that is, how the company intends to achieve its aims in the context within which it operates. We introduced business risks in Chapter 3. The company will implement strategies to avoid or manage any risk that it faces.

Measurement and review of the entity's financial performance

This is the company's monitoring of things that it considers to be important. For example, if the company has a strategy of sales to grow by 10% in the year, it will then have procedures to review how that strategy is being achieved. This may be:

- Reviewing sales levels per salesman on a month-by-month basis to see if there is steady growth

- Reviewing sales levels at the end of the year to see if the 10% target has been achieved

Speaking generally, an auditor prefers a company to take the first approach to review, as this step-by-step approach may allow the company to change its strategy or implement additional strategies during the year.

The second approach can create a situation where there is substantial pressure to achieve high targets towards the end of the year, which might lead to a temptation to report wrongly or even fraudulently.

The auditor is interested in the performance management side of an entity as it is an important aspect of the culture (control environment) of the company.

Why obtain an understanding of the entity and its environment?

Now we've looked at what auditors have to gain an understanding of, we'll look at why they have to gain such an understanding.

The basic answer is so that they know what the significant things in the financial statements are so that they can ensure that these items are thoroughly checked when seeking evidence to give their audit opinion.

Things are made significant by their importance to the entity, their complexity, the likelihood that they may have been misstated due to fraud or error. These things are what an auditor refers to as risks. I already mentioned that risk is very important to auditors. I'll tell you more about risk now.

AUDIT RISK

AUDIT RISK is the risk that the auditors give the inappropriate opinion as a result of their audit.

This may be that they have said that the financial statements give a true and fair view when they don't, or that the wrong reason has been given for why they do not give a true and fair view.

Audit risk is the chance that auditors might get it wrong. There are various factors in why they might get it wrong, and we examine these now.

Control risk

I will explain control risk first, because you should be so familiar with controls having looked at them for the last two chapters.

CONTROL RISK is the risk that the entity's internal control system will not prevent or detect and correct errors.

If an entity's controls are poor, then there is a strong chance that errors or frauds can occur when transactions and events are being recorded and that the financial statements, produced from the information system at the end of the year, will include those errors (known as misstatements).

If the financial statements contain lots of errors because they have been recorded wrongly from the very beginning, then there is quite a strong possibility that auditors will have difficulty finding those errors. This is control risk.

Remember that we said that auditors have to decide whether they think controls are effective or not, and if they think they are, they will choose to rely on them. In that instance, the auditors are saying control risk is low. In other words, that in their opinion, the control system does a good job in preventing or in detecting and correcting errors.

Inherent risk

INHERENT RISK is the risk that items will be misstated due to their nature or due to their context.

What does that mean? It means that things might be naturally risky. For example, walking a tightrope one metre above the ground is naturally less risky than walking a tightrope 101 metres above the ground.

In terms of financial statements, accounting for receivables is likely to be less risky than accounting for complicated group structures, because the accounting requirements are less complex for receivables.

Or, in terms of companies, sales is likely to be a more risky balance in a cash business than in a credit business. Why? Because cash, by its nature, is easy to lose or hide or steal. Therefore, recording cash sales is more risky than recording credit sales.

Detection risk

Control risk and inherent risk combined form the risk of misstatements appearing in the financial statements in the first place. These will affect the auditor's ability to find errors, because some errors may be difficult to discover.

However, auditors can usually control the overall level of audit risk by controlling the level of the last component of audit risk, which is detection risk.

DETECTION RISK is the risk that errors will exist in financial statements and the auditors will not discover them.

In other words, the auditors put together tests and enquiries to discover errors in the financial statements and they should be able to counter-balance the other risks by taking action. For example, if inherent and control risk is high, auditors need to undertake a lot of tests, and reduce the chance that they will fail to discover errors.

If there is only a low risk of errors existing in the financial statements in the first place, auditors can undertake fewer tests. This means that detection risk is increased, but as the other two elements of risk are lower, overall, the audit risk is acceptable.

HOW IT WORKS

If you like maths, this sum shows how this works mathematically and may help you. If you don't like maths, don't read this and get confused! Just read the explanation above.

AUDIT RISK = INHERENT RISK × CONTROL RISK × DETECTION RISK

ACCEPTABLE = INHERENT RISK × CONTROL RISK × ADJUSTABLE

So, for example, if:

INHERENT RISK = HIGH

CONTROL RISK = HIGH

Then DETECTION RISK needs to equal very low for overall audit risk to be acceptable.

$$\text{ACCEPTABLE} = \text{HIGH} \times \text{HIGH} \times \text{LOW}$$

When detection risk is set at low, the auditor needs to carry out **a lot of testing**. This is correct because the control system is poor and the business itself is 'risky' – so the auditor needs to carry out lots of tests to ensure that the risk of him missing something is low.

Or, if:

INHERENT RISK = HIGH

CONTROL RISK = LOW

Then DETECTION RISK can be medium.

$$\text{ACCEPTABLE} = \text{HIGH} \times \text{LOW} \times \text{MEDIUM}$$

The auditors have to apply various levels of judgement here:

(1)   What levels of risk leads to an overall acceptable level of risk?

(2)   What is control risk and inherent risk?

(3)   How much detection risk is acceptable?

(4)   How much and what work will reduce detection risk to an acceptable level?

Task 1

Select whether the following statements in respect of audit risk are true or false.

	Options
If inherent and control risk have been determined to be high, auditors will have to carry out a high level of testing to render overall audit risk acceptable.	True False
If inherent and control risk have been determined to be high, auditors will judge that detection risk must be low.	True False

MATERIALITY

Materiality is an important auditing concept which is closely linked with audit risk. ISA 200 *Overall Objectives of the Independent Auditor and the Conduct of an Audit in Accordance with International Standards on Auditing* states that, in general, misstatements are considered to be material if individually or in aggregate, they could reasonably be expected to influence the economic decisions of users, taken on the basis of the financial statements.

In other words, MATERIALITY is a measure of the significance of an item to financial statement users.

HOW IT WORKS

HEC's statement of financial position contains high levels of cash and receivables compared with inventory. It is likely that cash and receivables are material to the financial statements and inventory is not.

Calculation of materiality

The auditor must calculate a suitable level of materiality for the financial statements as a whole. This will often be a percentage of a significant benchmark in the financial statements. If you need to know a materiality level in the assessment, you will be given told the materiality level, or the benchmark (for example, 5% of profit before tax).

In addition, the auditor may need to calculate material levels for specific items in financial statements which are particularly significant to users for any reason. Some items might be material simply because of **what they are**. Because of the legal restrictions around directors' remuneration disclosures in the UK, any matter relating to directors in financial statements is usually considered to be material.

In addition, an error might be considered material because of **its effect**. For example, if a small error made the company breach a covenant made with its bank, it might be considered material.

Auditors must also calculate performance materiality. PERFORMANCE MATERIALITY is the amount or amounts set by the auditor at less than materiality for the financial statements as a whole. This reduces to an appropriately low level the probability that the aggregate of uncorrected and undetected misstatements exceeds materiality for the financial statements as a whole.

Individual items must not be considered in isolation. The auditors may find one error in inventory which they consider to be immaterial to the financial statements. However, they may also find a number of other immaterial errors in a range of account balances, all of which when added together, would have a material impact on the financial statements. Auditors must keep a record of immaterial errors they find and make an assessment whether together they need adjusting for.

Materiality may not stay the same during the audit, as information may come to light which causes the auditor to change his assessment of materiality. If this happens, the auditor should consider whether performance materiality requires adjusting too.

The auditor must document materiality and performance materiality in the audit strategy, and also note changes made during the audit, if relevant.

Materiality considerations during audit planning are particularly important. The assessment of materiality at this stage should be based on the most recent and reliable financial information and will help to determine an effective and efficient audit approach. Materiality assessment will help the auditors to decide:

- How many and what items to test
- Whether to use sampling techniques (see Chapter 6)
- What level of error is likely to lead to a modified audit opinion

The resulting combination of audit procedures should help to reduce audit risk to an appropriately low level. This is how risk and materiality are closely connected.

When devising tests, all items with a higher value than materiality should be tested.

Task 2

Select whether the following statements in respect of materiality are true or false.

	Options
Performance materiality should be set at less than materiality for the financial statements as a whole.	True False
Materiality is a measure of the importance of items to a reader of financial statements.	True False
Items may be material due to their size, nature or effect on the financial statements.	True False

Task 3

Select whether the following items are likely to be considered material or not material. Profit is £100,000 and materiality has been set at 5% of profit.

	Options
There is an error in receivables, value £7,500.	Material
	Not material
A loan to a director has been disclosed in the financial statement at £2,000. Actually the correct sum is £2,010.	Material
	Not material
The company is required to keep a current asset ratio of 2:1. An error of £100 has been found in receivables, which will cause the ratio to drop below this level.	Material
	Not material

ASSESSING AUDIT RISK

Assessing audit risk is an important job. We have already looked at assessing control risk and the responses that an auditor might take in response to control risk assessment. If controls are weak, his response (detection risk) is not to test controls. If controls are strong, his response is to test controls (he will have to determine how many tests to carry out in order to make detection risk an acceptable level).

We shall now look at assessing inherent risk.

Assessing inherent risk is also essentially a matter of auditor judgement. While obtaining their knowledge of the business, auditors will be identifying matters which may be risky for the audit.

Once risks have been identified, through the process of gaining an understanding of the entity, the auditor will relate the identified risks to what could go wrong at the financial statement level. He will consider if they are big enough to cause material misstatement and then consider the likelihood of the misstatement arising. He will also consider if any of the risks are significant risks.

Let's look at that in a step format:

Step 1 Identify inherent and control risks by gaining an understanding of the entity.

Step 2 Relate identified risks to what could go wrong at a financial statement level. (See below.)

Step 3   Consider if the risks are of a magnitude to cause material misstatement and how likely they are to arise.

Step 4   Consider if any identified risks are significant risks.

What could go wrong at a financial statement level?

- Items can be overstated

- Items can be understated or omitted

- Items can be disclosed wrongly or not disclosed at all

- Items can be accounted for wrongly (potentially causing over- or understatement)

HOW IT WORKS

The auditors might assess a risk that there is a customer who is making payments increasingly late, and has recently missed payment for some invoices altogether.

The impact that this could have on the financial statements is that **receivables could be overstated** if this customer does not intend or is not able to pay its outstanding balance.

Even though the client's books reasonably include the invoices owed by this client, there is a risk that the balance will not be paid and therefore the financial statements will be wrong by this amount.

Consider if risks will cause material misstatement and how likely they are to happen

The auditors use their knowledge of the business to assess whether potential misstatements are likely to be at the value they have determined is material.

Judging how likely risks are to arise will be a combination of auditor experience and common sense.

For example, some might consider that there is a risk that a meteor could hit a building owned by a client and that this would affect the valuation of non-current assets in the statement of financial position, but on balance, it's probably unlikely in the normal course of things

Some other risks might have a higher likelihood of arising. For example, if controls over cash at the client are weak, then there would be a high likelihood of sales being misstated (probably understated), as there is a good likelihood of an error arising as a result of weak controls.

Task 4

When planning an audit of financial statements, the external auditor is required to consider how factors such as the entity's operating environment and its system of internal control affect the risk of misstatement in the financial statements.

Select whether the following factors are likely to increase or reduce the risk of misstatement.

	Options
The entity is to be sold and the purchase consideration will be determined as a multiple of reported profit.	Increase Reduce
The company has a history of being slow to follow new accounting standards and guidance.	Increase Reduce

Consider if identified risks are significant risks

All identified risks which have a reasonable likelihood of causing a material misstatement in the financial statements should be subject to audit considerations and audit tests (we examine the auditor's response to risk assessment in the next chapters).

However, some risks may be so significant they require special audit considerations, and these are known as SIGNIFICANT RISKS.

SIGNIFICANT RISKS: FRAUD

The most relevant significant risk for our purposes is a risk of fraud.

HOW IT WORKS

There are various indicators of a risk of fraud.

Consider:

(1) Is management given incentive or pressurised into committing fraud?
(2) Is there opportunity to commit fraud?
(3) Do company attitudes permit fraud or are there other rationalisations?

Task 5

What factors might indicate that the answer to these questions is yes?

Auditors must evaluate the controls relevant to significant risks identified if they have not already done so.

So, when carrying out risk assessment procedures the auditors must consider the risk of fraud causing a misstatement in the financial statements.

Fraud can be defined as an intentional act by one or more individuals involving the use of deception to obtain an unjust or illegal advantage. It is different from error because fraud is intentional whereas errors are caused by mistake. Management and those charged with governance are primarily responsible for preventing and detecting fraud. It is up to them to place a strong emphasis within the company on fraud prevention.

The auditor's approach to the risk of fraud is similar to the approach to the risk of error we have been looking at. An overriding requirement for auditors is that they are alert to potential problems. The team must have **professional scepticism** and must **discuss the susceptibility of the financial statements to misstatement due to fraud**.

Auditors are required to make specific enquiries of management about the environment in the company in relation to fraud as part of obtaining an understanding of the entity. Auditors must also be conscious that risk of management fraud is greater than employee fraud, because management is in a position to conceal fraud by directly manipulating financial records or by overriding controls. As we saw in Chapter 3, assessing the control environment will be an important factor in assessing the risk of management fraud in terms of opportunity and incentive.

Auditors must consider general fraud risk factors. These might include the following.

- High turnover of key personnel
- Dominance of one member of the management team/dominant owner/ manager
- Frequent changes in advisers
- Management not taking holidays
- Understaffing in accounts department
- Inadequate working capital
- Industry volatility
- Time pressure to produce financial statements
- Performance-based remuneration
- Weak control environment
- Unreliable information
- Management overriding controls

If the auditors think that fraud exists they should:

- Carry out extra/different procedures

- Document their findings

- Report it to the appropriate level of management (or a third party if there is a legal duty to do so)

- Consider its impact on the rest of the audit

We look at reporting on fraud in Chapter 10.

Summary

(1) Auditors determine overall responses to risk assessment and incorporate these in the audit strategy.

(2) Auditors determine an overall audit approach in terms of whether they are going to test controls and reduce detailed testing, or not rely on controls and carry out substantial detailed testing.

(3) Auditors determine responses to individual risks according to that audit approach (see Chapters 6 to 9). Whether they test both controls and balances and transactions in detail, or just balances and transactions in detail, they will always carry out tests of detail on material items.

(4) Auditors must be alert to the risk of fraud

Task 6

When planning an audit of financial statements, the external auditor is required to consider how factors such as the entity's operating environment and its system of internal control affect the risk of misstatement in the financial statements.

Select whether the following factors are likely to increase or reduce the risk of misstatement.

	Options
The entity is committed to employing skilled personnel in the accounts department.	Increase Reduce
The company prepares detailed budgets and analyses variances from budgets closely.	Increase Reduce
The entity's management has not remedied deficiencies in internal control noted by the auditors in the past.	Increase Reduce

CHAPTER OVERVIEW

- The auditor is required by auditing standards to gain an understanding of the entity and its environment. This includes:

    - External factors
    - Internal factors
    - Internal control
    - Performance measurement

- They obtain an understanding to enable audit judgements and to assess risk

- Auditors must reduce overall audit risk to an acceptable level

- This is done by adjusting detection risk, the only part of the risk equation which the auditors can directly influence

- Detection risk is affected by the types of test carried out and the number of tests carried out

- Auditors assess where audit risks arise and evaluate how they will impact the financial statements

- They assess if risks are likely to cause material misstatements

- They will also assess if any of the risks are significant risks

- Auditors must be aware of the possibility of misstatements in the financial statements due to fraud

Keywords

Stakeholders – people with an interest in the company

Audit risk – the risk that the auditors give the wrong opinion as a result of their audit

Control risk – the risk that the entity's internal control system will not prevent or detect and correct errors

Inherent risk – the risk that items will be misstated due to their nature or due to their context

Detection risk – the risk that errors will exist in financial statements and the auditors will not discover them

Materiality – a measure of the significance of an item to financial statement users

Performance materiality – the amount or amounts set by the auditor at less than materiality for the financial statements as a whole to reduce to an appropriately low level the probability that the aggregate of uncorrected and undetected misstatements exceeds materiality for the financial statements as a whole.

Significant risks are risks that require special audit consideration

TEST YOUR LEARNING

Test 1 Complete the statement. The auditors must gain an understanding of the following areas of a business:

....

....

....

....

....

Test 2 Which of the following statements best summarises why auditors must gain an understanding of the entity?

In order to understand internal control systems ☐

In order to be able to assess risks ☐

In order to see what items there are to be audited ☐

In order to eliminate items from testing ☐

Test 3 Complete the definitions using the items in the pick list below.

.... risk is the risk that the auditors give an .... opinion on the financial statements.

.... risk is the risk that the entity's internal control system will not prevent or detect and correct errors

.... risk is the risk that items will be misstated due to their .... or due to their ....

.... risk is the risk that errors will exist in financial statements and the auditors will not discover them

Pick list

Incorrect

Audit

Context

Inherent

Inappropriate

Detection

Control

Nature

Test 4 Select whether the following statements are True or False.

	Options
Auditors cannot affect inherent and control risk as inherent and control risks are the risks that errors will arise in the financial statements as a result of control problems or the nature of items in the financial statements of the entity. The auditors cannot control those factors.	True False
If inherent and control risk are high, detection risk should be rendered low to come to an overall acceptable level of risk. In order for detection risk to be low, the auditors will have to carry out a lower level of testing.	True False

Test 5 When planning an audit of financial statements, the auditor is required to consider how factors such as the entity's operating environment and its system of control affect the risk of material misstatement in the financial statements.

Select whether the following factors are likely to increase or reduce the risk of misstatement.

	Options
The control environment is weak and there is considerable pressure on management to improve results year-on-year.	Increase Reduce
Management has implemented improvements in controls as a result of weaknesses identified last year.	Increase Reduce

Test 6 Select whether the following statements in respect of materiality are true.

	Options
Materiality is the concept of significance to users of the financial statements.	True False
Performance materiality will usually be higher than materiality assessed for the financial statements as a whole.	True False

Test 7 When planning an audit of financial statements, the auditor is required to consider how factors such as the entity's nature and operating environment affect the risk of material misstatement in the financial statements.

Select whether the following factors are likely to increase or reduce the risk of misstatement.

	Options
The company has diversified its operations during the year.	Increase Reduce
The company has discontinued operations in its riskiest operating area during the year.	Increase Reduce

chapter 6:
AUDIT PLANNING

chapter coverage 📖

Once the auditors have assessed risks and started determining the audit approach, as I said in the previous chapter, the auditors will put together an audit strategy and plan. I'll outline the contents of an audit plan in this chapter and also give you a few more details about items included in the plan, for example, the audit sample.

The topics covered are:

✍ The audit strategy document

✍ Responding to the risk assessment (audit plan)

✍ Audit sampling

THE AUDIT STRATEGY DOCUMENT

Auditors are required by auditing standards to plan their audit so as to perform the audit in an effective manner.

Planning will:

- Ensure that appropriate attention is devoted to different areas of the audit
- Ensure that potential problems are identified
- Allow proper assignment of work to engagement team members
- Make the review process easier

The AUDIT STRATEGY is the document outlining the general approach to the audit which gives direction to the audit and sets out its scope and conduct. It incorporates overall responses to the risk assessment (which are set out later in this chapter).

The planning meeting

The audit team will have a planning meeting to discuss the audit strategy and so that the audit engagement partner can outline to each member of the team what his responsibilities are. He will also take the opportunity to inform the team of any issues they should be aware of, confidential matters, and to remind them of their duty of professional scepticism.

PROFESSIONAL SCEPTICISM is the attitude of critical assessment and the use of a questioning mind necessary to prevent overlooking suspicious circumstances or from drawing incorrect conclusions. The auditor should neither assume that management is dishonest nor fail to question whether they are honest.

The audit team is also required to discuss the susceptibility of the financial statements to error and fraud and the risks in the audit. This can be done at the planning meeting.

RESPONDING TO THE RISK ASSESSMENT (AUDIT PLAN)

The auditor must respond to the risk assessment in two ways:

- Overall responses
- Individual responses

Overall responses

The auditors will look at the overall risks in the audit and will devise overall strategies to combat them. Such responses will include:

- Reminding the audit team of their duty to do their work with professional scepticism (for example, at the planning meeting)

- Assigning more experienced staff to the team

- Providing more supervision for staff on the team

- Using staff with special skills

- Incorporating additional elements of uncertainty into the audit procedures

Individual responses

The auditors will also come up with individual responses to specific risks in the form of audit procedures. Determining the audit procedures that will be carried out is called putting together an audit plan. An AUDIT PLAN is a list of the detailed procedures that will be carried out to gain evidence to give an opinion on the financial statements.

AUDIT EVIDENCE is all the information used by the auditor in arriving at the conclusions on which the auditor's opinion is based.

Auditing standards require auditors to obtain **sufficient** and **appropriate** audit evidence.

Auditors are required to carry out tests of detail (substantive tests) on material items.

Procedures to collect evidence

I already outlined the kinds of procedures that you would carry out to test controls. Auditors use similar procedures to test balances and transactions in detail. This is the full list of procedures auditors might use:

- Inspecting records or documents (inspection)

- Inspecting tangible assets (inspection)

- Making enquiries of staff (enquiry)

- Looking at client staff operating the system (**observation**)

- Confirming items with parties outside the organisation (external confirmation)

- Recalculating items (recalculation)

- Redoing control procedures, to ensure they were done properly, for example, reconciliations (this type of test is called **reperformance**)

- Analytical procedures

The procedure that probably needs the most explanation is analytical procedures.

Analytical procedures

ANALYTICAL PROCEDURES include:

(a) The **consideration of comparisons** of this year's financial information with:

    (i) Similar information for prior periods

    (ii) Anticipated results of the client

    (iii) Predictions prepared by the auditors

    (iv) Industry information, such as a comparison of the client's ratio of sales to trade receivables with industry averages, or with the ratios relating to other entities of comparable size in the same industry

(b) Those between **elements of financial information** that are **expected to conform** to a predicted pattern based on experience, such as the relationship of gross profit to sales

(c) Those between **financial information** and **relevant non-financial information**, such as the relationship of payroll costs to number of employees

A variety of methods can be used to perform these procedures, ranging from simple comparisons to complex analysis using statistics, on a company level, branch level or individual account level. The choice of procedures is a matter for the auditors' professional judgement.

Using analytical procedures

Auditors are required to use analytical procedures as part of the risk assessment process at the planning stage of the audit, to:

- Identify risk areas
- Determine the nature, timing and extent of procedures

The auditor may also use analytical procedures as substantive procedures.

There are a number of factors which the auditors should consider when deciding whether to use analytical procedures as substantive procedures, such as:

- Whether the procedures are **suitable** to obtain evidence about the relevant assertions (given the assessed risk for those assertions)
- Whether the data the auditor is using is:
  - **Reliable**
  - **Available**
  - **Relevant**

Investigating significant fluctuations or unexpected relationships

When analytical procedures identify significant fluctuations or unexpected relationships the auditors must investigate by obtaining adequate explanations from management and appropriate corroborative evidence.

Investigations will start with **enquiries** to management and then **confirmation** of management's responses.

HOW IT WORKS

When carrying out analytical procedures, auditors should remember that every industry is different and each company within an industry differs in certain respects.

Significant items

Payables and purchases

Inventory and cost of sales

Non-current assets and depreciation, repairs and maintenance expense

Intangible assets and amortisation

Loans and interest expense

Investments and investment income

Receivables and irrecoverable receivables expense

Receivables and sales

Important accounting ratios

$$\text{Gross profit margin} = \frac{\text{Gross profit}}{\text{Revenue}} \times 100\%$$

This should be calculated in total and by product, area and month/quarter if possible.

$$\text{Receivables turnover period} = \frac{\text{Receivables}}{\text{Revenue}} \times 365$$

$$\text{Inventory turnover ratio} = \frac{\text{Cost of sales}}{\text{Inventory}}$$

$$\text{Current ratio} = \frac{\text{Current assets}}{\text{Current liabilities}}$$

$$\text{Quick or acid test ratio} = \frac{\text{Current assets (excluding inventory)}}{\text{Current liabilities}}$$

$$\text{Gearing ratio} = \frac{\text{Loans}}{\text{Share capital and reserves}} \times 100\%$$

$$\text{Return on capital employed} = \frac{\text{Profit before tax}}{\text{Total assets} - \text{Current liabilities}}$$

You should be familiar with these ratios from your other studies. Remember ratios mean very little when used in isolation. They should be **calculated for previous periods** and for **comparable companies**. Audit working papers should contain summarised accounts and the chosen ratios for prior years. In addition to looking at the more usual ratios, the auditors should consider examining **other ratios** that may be **relevant** to the particular **clients' business**, such as revenue per passenger mile for an airline operator client, or fees per partner for a professional office.

One further important technique is to examine **important related accounts** in conjunction with each other. It is often the case that revenue and expense accounts are related to statement of financial position accounts and comparisons should be made to ensure that the relationships are reasonable. These relationships have been listed above.

Task 1

The external auditor is required to undertake analytical procedures as part of the planning process in order to identify the risk of misstatement of figures in the financial statements. The results of the analytical procedures conducted on trade receivables and trade payables in the financial statements of an audit client are listed below.

Select whether the results indicate that trade receivables and trade payables may have been under-, or overstated.

The results show that, compared to the previous year:

	Options
Trade receivables has increased by 25% and revenue has increased by 7%.	Understated
	Overstated
Trade payables has decreased by 5% and purchases has increased by 4%	Understated
	Overstated

Task 2

Auditors use tests of controls and substantive procedures to gather audit evidence.

For each of the procedures listed below, select whether it is a test of control or a substantive procedure.

	Options
Inspecting purchase orders for evidence that the additions and calculations have been checked.	Test of control Substantive procedure
Recalculating a depreciation charge.	Test of control Substantive procedure
Comparing month on month sales to the previous year.	Test of control Substantive procedure

Financial statement assertions

Tests of detail (substantive tests) are tests based upon the financial statement assertions.

The FINANCIAL STATEMENT ASSERTIONS are the claims (or assertions) made by the directors in putting together the financial statements. For example, by including a non-current asset in the financial statements, the directors are claiming that it exists. They are claiming it has a certain value and are claiming it belongs to the company.

ISA 315 *Identifying and Assessing The Risks of Material Misstatement Through Understanding The Entity and Its Environment* states that there are three categories of assertion:

-   Assertions about classes of transactions and events for the period under audit (occurrence, completeness, accuracy, cut-off and classification)

-   Assertions about account balances at the period end (existence, rights and obligations, completeness, valuation and allocation)

-   Assertions about presentation and disclosure (occurrence and rights and obligations, completeness, classification and understandability and accuracy and valuation)

These can be defined as:

– **Occurrence** – transactions and events disclosed in the financial statements have occurred.

– **Completeness** – all transactions, events, assets, liabilities, equity interests and disclosures that should have been included in the financial statements have been.

– **Accuracy** – amounts and other information relating to the transaction have been recorded appropriately.

– **Cut-off** – transactions and events have been recorded in the correct accounting period.

– **Classification/understandability** – transactions and events are recorded in the right accounts and disclosures are clearly expressed.

– **Existence** – assets and liabilities exist.

– **Rights and obligations** – the entity holds or controls the rights to assets and liabilities are the obligations of the entity, transactions pertain to the entity.

– **Valuation** (and allocation) – assets, liabilities and equity interests are valued correctly.

So the tests that auditors plan as a result of the risk assessment procedures are designed to test the relevant assertions relating to that balance, transaction or disclosure. We shall see examples of specific substantive tests in Chapters 7 to 9.

One important matter is the 'direction' of a test. If auditors are testing whether something has been **understated** in the financial statements, they must start the test at a source document (such as an order, or requisition). If auditors are testing whether something has been **overstated** in the financial statements, they start with ledger accounts and trace back to source documents – to ensure the item existed in the first place.

Task 3

As part of verification techniques in respect of non-current assets additions, an auditor will inspect a hire purchase agreement. The auditor will gain assurance about different assertions depending on the information given in the agreement.

In respect of the information below, select the assertion for which that information will provide evidence.

	Options
Terms of the agreement.	Rights and obligations Existence Valuation
Total amount on the agreement.	Rights and obligations Existence Valuation

In addition to deciding what tests to do, the auditors have to determine how many items to test. Auditors often use a sample, and we look at the issue of sampling next.

AUDIT SAMPLING

AUDIT SAMPLING is applying audit procedures to less than 100% of items within an account balance or class of transactions in such a way as to draw a conclusion on the account balance or class of transactions as a whole.

STATISTICAL SAMPLING is an approach to sampling that involves random selection of the sample items; and the use of probability theory to evaluate sample results including measurement of sampling risk. A sampling approach that does not have these characteristics is considered non-statistical sampling.

The key rule of audit sampling is that all 'sampling units' must have an equal chance of being selected for testing

SAMPLING UNITS are the individual items constituting a 'population' (account balance or class of transaction), for example, a single receivable balance within total receivables or an individual sale within total revenue (turnover).

As you may have gathered, sampling is closely connected with risk and materiality. Sampling affects detection risk because, put simply, the more items within a population that are tested, the higher the chance of the auditor finding an error. Hence detection risk is lowered.

However, this is made more complex by the fact that sampling by its nature increases detection risk as, if not everything is tested, there is a risk that errors will not be detected. However carefully it is selected, it is possible that the sample will not be representative of the population as a whole.

Sampling is therefore a risk. The auditor has to determine an appropriate level of this risk in order to obtain the benefit of sampling (which is that auditors don't have to test everything!).

Non-sampling techniques

In some instances, auditors will want to exercise judgement and test specific items rather than selecting a sample.

For instance, we have already observed that auditors should test all material items. Therefore, if the receivables' ledger contains debts that are themselves material to the financial statements, they should be selected.

This is not a sample by the above definition. Because these items have been selected with bias, the auditor cannot assume that they are reflective of the rest of the population, and should not project the results of testing on these items to the rest of the population.

The remainder of the population should be sampled in a non-biased way. This is known as stratifying a population. STRATIFICATION is dividing a population into mini-populations, usually by value.

Therefore, instead of testing receivables as a whole, the auditor might test two populations of receivable balances, individually material receivable balances and individually non-material receivable balances (the total of which might well be material).

In this circumstance, the auditor would not apply sampling procedures to the first population, and would instead test all of the material balances. The auditor would apply sampling procedures to the second population and select balances for testing. Results from the sampled population could be projected onto the rest of that mini-population to assess if total misstatements are likely to be material.

In the first population, there would be no need to project results, because if everything has been tested, there is nothing to project the errors against. All errors in that population should have been found.

In some audit areas, it might be more appropriate to test 100% of items, or a very high percentage of items (so that errors in the remaining balance couldn't possibly be material). An example is often additions to property, plant and equipment, where only one or two material additions may have been made in the year, and there is no need to select a sample, merely to test these items.

Sampling techniques, in many areas of the financial statements, is necessary, because it is the only cost effective way an audit can be performed (testing everything would take too long and be too expensive). The size of samples selected will be affected by the auditor's assessment of the tolerable misstatement.

For tests of control, the tolerable misstatement is the maximum rate of deviation from a control that auditors are willing to accept in the population and still conclude that the preliminary assessment of control risk is valid.

For tests of details, the tolerable misstatement is the maximum monetary error in an account balance or class of transactions that the auditor is willing to accept and still conclude that the financial statements are true and fair.

Confidence level

In other words, the auditor has to reach an appropriate confidence level. When using a sample, he has to be sufficiently confident that the results given by a sample reflect the results that would be given by testing the whole population.

If overall risk of misstatement is high, the auditor needs to be very confident that the results from a sample reflect the results that would come from the whole population. This would increase the size of the sample size. All this is a matter of auditor judgement based on the risks of errors arising and materiality levels. This sort of judgement is taken at the planning stage and amended, if necessary, as the audit progresses and more facts come to light. It is taken by a senior member of the audit team and approved by the audit partner.

The auditing standard on audit sampling, ISA 530 *Audit Sampling* outlines factors that impact on sample sizes, and these are summarised below.

Factor	Effect on sample size for tests of controls
Increase in extent to which auditor intends to rely on controls	**Increase** – because the more reliance the auditor intends to place on controls, the greater his assurance they are operating effectively needs to be.
Increase in the tolerable rate of deviation	**Decrease**
Increase in the expected rate of deviation	**Increase** – because if auditors expect errors to exist, they need to test more as they need to be satisfied that actual error is lower than tolerable error.
Increase in the auditor's desired level of assurance that actual rate of deviation ≤tolerable rate of deviation	**Increase** – because the more assurance the auditor needs, the more items he needs to test.
Increase of number of sampling units	**Negligible effect**

Factor	Effect on sample size for tests of detail
Increase in auditor's assessment of the risk of material misstatement	**Increase** – because the higher inherent and control risk is, the lower detection risk needs to be (hence more tests).
Increase in the use of other procedures at the same assertion	**Decrease** – because the auditor is obtaining assurance from the other procedures (for example, analytical procedures).
Increase in the auditor's desired level of assurance that actual misstatement ≤ tolerable misstatement	**Increase** – because the more assurance the auditor needs, the more items he needs to test.
Increase in tolerable misstatement	**Decrease** – because there is more chance of it being found in the sample
Increase in expected misstatement	**Increase** – because if auditors expect more errors to exist, they need to test more as they need to be satisfied that actual misstatement is lower than tolerable misstatement.
Stratification of the population	**Decrease**
Number of sampling units in population	**Negligible effect**

How to pick the sample

The important rule above comes in here. It is important that any item in the population has a chance of being picked – so, in general terms, the auditor should not bias the sample.

For example, if a company has two factories, one 20 miles from the auditor and one 120 miles from the auditor, it is easier for the auditor to physically verify that the closer one exists. However, this would be putting an unreasonable bias on the sample selection.

In order to avoid bias, there are several common ways of selecting samples:

(1) By **random numbers**. The auditor uses a computer programme or table to (mathematically) randomly select the sample.

(2) By **systematic selection**. The auditor randomly selects the first item and then selects all the others systematically after that. For example, the auditor might pick the fifth debtor on the list of debts and then every fifth or tenth after that.

(3) By **haphazard selection**. This is the approach most likely to allow audit bias to creep in. This is a method by which an auditor picks a sample

with no structured technique (that is, what we would call 'at random' although human bias may reduce the mathematical randomness of the choice).It is crucial that you understand the difference between this type of sampling and 'random' sampling, outlined above.

(4) By **Money Unit Sampling (MUS)** which is a value-weighted selection, so that (for example, in trade receivables), every nth £ is selected, rather than every nth receivable.

(5) By **block selection** which involves selecting a block of continuous items (for example, April's invoices out of a population of the year's invoices). This is rarely an appropriate sample technique, as April's invoices may have different characteristics from the rest of the year and are not therefore representative of the whole population (for example, if they were posted by a different staff member due to holiday).

HOW IT WORKS

HEC's sales ledger contains three receivables with material balances at the year-end and 15 other, non-material balances (materiality has been set at £6,000):

	£
Abbott Guest House	1,046
Briers, The	978
Dell, The	445
Elms, The	596
Grand Hotel, The	10,593
Graveleas	299
Happy Eatin'	9,967
Homelea	924
Jade Garden	4,355
Laurels, The	377
Morningside Guest House	89
Natura	3,296
Paradiso	268
Quinn's Fine Dining	2,831
Secret Garden	6,898
Smallville Hotel	5,709
Turners'	311
Victorine's	1,936
	50,918

In this instance, then, the auditors could stratify the sales ledger into material balances which will all be tested and non-material balances which will be sampled. You can see that the second population is still material in total.

	£
Grand Hotel, The	10,593
Happy Eatin'	9,967
Secret Garden	6,898
	27,458

	£
Abbott Guest House	1,046
Briers, The	978
Dell, The	445
Elms, The	596
Graveleas	299
Homelea	924
Jade Garden	4,355
Laurels, The	377
Morningside Guest House	89
Natura	3,296
Paradiso	268
Quinn's Fine Dining	2,831
Smallville Hotel	5,709
Turners'	311
Victorine's	1,936
	23,460

The sample size for the second population has been set at five. This sample is most likely to be picked in one of the following two ways:

(1) Systematically (there are 15 balances, so intervals of three makes sense). Say the haphazardly picked starting point was the second balance, this would give the following sample:

	£
Briers, The	978
Graveleas	299
Laurels, The	377
Paradiso	268
Turners'	311
	2,233

Say the haphazardly picked starting point was the sixth balance, this would give the following sample:

	£
Homelea	924
Morningside Guest House	89
Quinn's Fine Dining	2,831
Victorine's	1,936
Dell, The	445
	6,225

Note that these two sample selections give a different total coverage in terms of **value**. This does not matter. Because the sample has been picked without bias, the sample should be reflective of the population. The calculations that have gone into determining the sample size in the first place mean that value is now irrelevant.

(2) The sample could also be picked completely haphazardly (for example, by the auditor putting his pen on the paper five times with his eyes shut!). However, when selecting haphazardly, the auditor should take care not to be biased by anything (for example, value, or by auditor knowledge about the customers – for example, that a particular customer has historically not replied to the auditors when they have sought confirmation of the balance).

Task 4

Determination of sample sizes on an audit is a judgemental matter. Using the options given below, outline the impact the following matters have on the sample sizes for tests of controls.

	Options
Auditors intend to increase reliance on the company's system of internal control for the purposes of the audit.	Increase Decrease No effect
Auditors believe that there is likely to be a higher deviation rate in controls due to a new member of staff.	Increase Decrease No effect
Increased activity in the factory and new customers, resulting in 25% more sales invoices being issued during the year.	Increase Decrease No effect

Task 5

The objective of a substantive test will determine the population from which the sample is selected.

For each of the objectives set out below, select the population from which the sample should be selected.

	Options
Obtain evidence that sales have not been understated.	Sales order
	Sales ledger
Obtain evidence that sales have not been overstated.	Sales order
	Sales ledger

CHAPTER OVERVIEW

- Auditors are required to plan audits so as to conduct them in an efficient manner

- The audit strategy will be discussed in an audit planning meeting, where the staff can also discuss the risk of material misstatement in the financial statements

- Auditors need to obtain sufficient and appropriate audit evidence about identified risks which could cause material misstatements

- The auditors response to risks will be overall responses in the audit strategy in individual responses of planned audit procedures (audit plan)

- The audit plan contains details of tests that will be carried out for each account balance or class of transaction. Auditors usually use a sample rather than testing every item in financial statements

- Sampling increases detection risk because errors in the population may not be sampled

- Auditors have to ensure that they have an appropriate 'confidence level' that the sample is reflective of the population as a whole in terms of errors

- Samples should be picked without bias

- Auditors should test individually material items

- Auditors try to ensure avoidance of bias when picking samples by using random number tables, systematic, haphazard, monetary unit or block sequence selection

Keywords

Audit strategy – the document outlining the general approach to the audit which gives direction to the audit and sets out the scope and conduct for the audit

Professional scepticism – the attitude of critical assessment and the use of a questioning mind necessary to prevent overlooking suspicious circumstances or from drawing incorrect conclusions

Audit plan – a list of the detailed procedures that will be carried out to gain evidence to give an opinion on the financial statements

Audit evidence – all the information used by the auditor in arriving at the conclusions on which the audit opinion is based

Analytical procedures – evaluations of financial information made by a study of financial and non-financial data

Financial statement assertions – the claims (or assertions) made by the directors in putting together the financial statements

Audit sampling – applying audit procedures to less than 100% of items within an account balance or class of transactions in such a way as to draw a conclusion on the account balance or class of transactions as a whole

Statistical sampling – an approach to sampling that involves random selection of the sample items and the use of probability theory to evaluate sample results including measurement of sampling risk. A sampling approach that does not have these characteristics is considered non-statistical sampling

Sampling units – the individual items constituting a 'population' (account balance or class of transaction), for example, a single receivable balance within total receivables or an individual sale within total revenue (turnover)

Stratification – dividing a population into mini-populations, usually by value

TEST YOUR LEARNING

Test 1 Complete the following definitions by filling in the gaps using the items in the pick list below.

The audit .... is the document that contains the general approach to the audit

The audit .... is the document that contains the details of tests that will be carried out for each .... or

....

.... is an attitude of .... that assumes neither honesty or dishonesty on the part of the directors but allows the auditor to observe and interpret relevant information as it becomes available to them during the audit.

Pick list

Strategy

Account balance

Financial statements

Plan

Programme

Class of transactions

Professional scepticism

Awareness

Knowledge

Test 2 State whether the following statements are True or False in respect of the audit engagement.

	Options
At an audit team meeting the audit partner must emphasise the importance of professional scepticism.	True False
An audit team must have a planning meeting only if the assessed risks are higher than anticipated.	True False

Test 3 Which of the following is not an overall response to risk assessment?

- Assigning more experienced staff to an audit ☐
- Reminding the team of their duty of professional scepticism ☐
- Formulating audit procedures in an audit plan ☐
- Incorporating elements of uncertainty into the audit process ☐

Test 4 When designing further audit procedures as a result of risk assessment, auditors design tests which give evidence about financial statement assertions. Select which category each assertion is relevant to.

	Options
Existence	Classes of transaction
	Account balance
	Presentation and disclosure
Valuation and allocation	Classes of transaction
	Account balance
	Presentation and disclosure
Cut-off	Classes of transaction
	Account balance
	Presentation and disclosure

Test 5 Which of the following statements is the important general rule concerning audit sampling?

- All sampling units should have an equal chance of being selected for testing ☐
- All audit areas must be subject to sampling ☐
- Auditors must always stratify a population to focus attention on high value items ☐
- The more items there are in a population, the higher the sample sizes must be ☐

Test 6 When using sampling techniques, auditors must select a sample such that each individual sampling unit is capable of being selected. Using the options provided below, select which method of sampling will be most suitable in each instance described.

	Options
Simran has been asked to select a sample of 12 sales invoices to trace from sales order to general ledger. There are 16 folders of sales orders for the year, stored in the sales office.	Random Systematic Haphazard
Julie has been asked to select a sample of five purchase ledger accounts to carry out a supplier statement reconciliation. There are 16 purchase ledger accounts.	Random Systematic Haphazard
Ben is selecting a sample of inventory lines to perform a valuation test. The audit team has been instructed to use the computerised techniques available to them, one of which is a sample selection programme.	Random Systematic Haphazard

Test 7 Determination of sample sizes on an audit is a judgemental matter. Using the options provided below, outline the impact the following matters have on the sample sizes for audit tests.

	Options
Increase in the auditor's assessment of the risk of material misstatement.	Increase Decrease No effect
Increase in tolerable misstatement.	Increase Decrease No effect
Decision to stratify a large population.	Increase Decrease No effect

chapter 7:
AUDIT OF INVENTORY

chapter coverage 📖

I've already mentioned several times that auditors will always carry out some tests of detail of transactions and balances (substantive tests) in an audit. In this chapter we introduce the tests that auditors carry out over a balance that, particularly in manufacturing companies, can be a highly material balance: inventory, sometimes known in the UK as stock.

The topics covered are:

✍ Introduction to inventory

✍ Existence of inventory

✍ Cut off of inventory

✍ Valuation of inventory

INTRODUCTION TO INVENTORY

Inventory can be a difficult balance for auditors to audit. Can you think why inventory might be difficult for auditors to audit?

There are various reasons. Closing inventory appears on both the statement of financial position and in the statement of comprehensive income and can have a significant impact on profit. It is often material to both of these statements. Also, inventory does not always form part of the normal accounting records. It is usually counted at the year end and added into the overall financial statements by a journal entry. This means that errors in inventory are not likely to be uncovered by other testing, as may be the case in other areas (for example – errors in receivables will probably also highlight errors in sales due to the double entry connection between them).

In Chapter 6 we outlined that substantive tests are concerned with financial statement assertions. The assertions that are most important with regard to inventory are existence, cut-off and valuation.

Existence

The key risk related to auditing the existence of inventory is the nature of the inventory.

Task 1

State whether the following statement is True or False.

	Options
The risk associated with the existence of inventory is an inherent risk.	True
	False

Inventory is very often a large number of relatively small or low value items. It may be held in a number of different locations.

The problems are as follows:

- Inventory may be easy to steal or lose

- Inventory may be difficult to count/ascertain and specialist help might be required

- Inventory may be in transit between locations

- It may not be possible to count inventory on the relevant day (a reconciliation to the correct day might be required)

- Inventory counters may be over familiar with the inventory and not count it properly

- It may be necessary to estimate the quantity of some items of inventory

HOW IT WORKS

Use MEM as an example. The company produces metal extrusions. There are 500 different types of extrusion, which range from 2mm extrusions to 50cm ones. The company keeps finished goods in the warehouse, on the factory floor when there is not room in the warehouse, the production director keeps a number of lines in his office, the sales team have a selection in their office, and one of MEM's customers maintains a small inventory of MEM products which they only buy if they use.

Task 2

Set out why it might be difficult to audit the existence of inventory at MEM.

Completeness

The problems of ensuring that inventory is recorded completely are clearly linked to the problems of existence and cut-off.

It is hugely important to get the 'cut-off' of inventory right, so that goods which have been despatched and counted in sales are not doubled-counted by still being included in inventory, or goods which have been delivered by suppliers are not included in inventory but omitted from purchases. Such cut-off problems would overstate profit.

The best way to achieve correct inventory cut-off is to shut down operations when the inventory is being counted so that there are no movements of inventory on the day. However, this is not always practical for companies. If it is not practical for companies to stop operations, they should implement strict controls over operations for that day to try and prevent cut-off problems arising.

Valuation

The problem of inventory valuation follows on from the problems of existence. Clearly if there is a large number of different inventory items, they are likely to be valued differently, and the material total for inventory in the financial statements may well comprise a large number of individually immaterial items. This can lead to high sample sizes.

In addition, the auditor needs to be sure that inventory is correctly valued according to the law and accounting standards, according to the lower of cost and net realisable value rule.

A problem with net realisable value is that inventory may go out of date, or become damaged and its value may be affected. So the auditor needs not only to be sure that the existence of inventory is correct, but that identified inventory is of good enough quality to justify its value (in other words, the inventory must not be obsolete).

In addition, work in progress and finished goods may be difficult to value as it may be difficult to assess cost when it includes the cost of making the inventory into what it is (including labour costs and general overheads of running the factory). The auditors may also assess the level of completeness of work in progress and assess whether the 'partial' valuation applied is reasonable.

HOW IT WORKS

At MEM, production processes are very short, so 'work in progress' only exists while a process is being carried out. As the factory shuts down on the last day of the year in order to count the inventory, there is never any work in progress at the year end.

MEM estimates the cost of finished goods by applying a standard unit cost for labour and factory overheads to the cost of materials. This standard cost is recalculated by Marie Edgehill on an annual basis by reference to the costs of manufacturing labour from the payroll and on specified factory costs for the year. Given that there is very little difference in the time the process takes for each item of inventory, regardless of its size, the standard cost is applied equally to each item.

Task 3

When testing the valuation of finished goods at MEM, set out what factors the auditors will need to consider.

EXISTENCE OF INVENTORY

Remember that the directors are responsible for discovering how much inventory the company has at the year end date in order to include this inventory in the financial statements. The auditors are concerned with verifying that this amount is correct.

The directors will usually carry out a inventory count (sometimes known as an stocktake) at the year end date in order to determine the levels of inventory.

The count might not be at the year end if:

(a) It is **not possible to stop factory operations** in order to allow the count to take place and the **count needs to be conducted at a different time** (say at a weekend). If this is the case, the directors will **substantiate** the amount of inventory at the count date and then perform a **reconciliation** to the correct date by adjusting for sales, purchases and factory activity. The reliability of results in this situation will be affected by:

   - The length of time between the inventory count and the year end

   - The effectiveness of the business's system of internal controls

   - The quality of records of inventory movements in the period between the inventory count and the year end

(b) The company operates a **perpetual inventory system** and could tell you at any time of year what levels of inventory exist. If this is the case, the company is likely to carry out inventory counts at least annually to **check that the system is operating effectively**, but these counts will not have to be at the year end. The count is **not substantiating the amount of inventory**, but checking that the controls over inventory operate effectively. Adequate inventory records will need to be maintained and kept up to date including any adjustments required following the inventory count. The auditor might attend such a count, but would be testing controls only, not carrying out any tests of detail.

When inventory is material in the financial statements, auditors are required to attend the inventory count and obtain audit evidence about the existence of inventory and its condition, unless it is impracticable for them to do so.

If it is impracticable for them to attend, they must consider alternative procedures, or it may not be possible for them to give an opinion on the truth and fairness of the financial statements with regard to inventory.

Planning attendance at a inventory count

The auditor usually attends the inventory count to carry out a combination of tests of controls and substantive tests.

(a) **Tests of controls**. The auditor will want to ensure that the controls the company has in place over counting the inventory are capable of ensuring that inventory is counted correctly and are operated efficiently.

(b) **Substantive tests**. The auditor will want to observe the condition of inventory being counted and identify any inventory which is obsolete or damaged. He/she will want to identify some inventory being counted to trace later to final inventory sheets to ensure that all items counted on the day are included in financial statements. The auditor may want to assess the degree of completion of any work in progress. He/she may also want to isolate the last deliveries to and from the company before the inventory count to assist in cut-off testing.

It is usually best if staff members who are familiar with the company and its inventory are sent to attend inventory counts. Prior to attendance, the auditor should:

- Review prior year working papers to become familiar with the arrangements

- Discuss the arrangements for the count with the person in charge of the count at the company

- Assess the key factors relating to the count (where most of the inventories are, what the high value items are)

- Review the company's inventory count instructions to assess whether they indicate that controls are sufficient to ensure inventories are counted correctly

- Plan the procedures to be carried out

Controls over the inventory count

The management of the company should ensure that there are adequate controls over the organisation of the count, over counting itself and over recording.

(a) **Organisation**: Senior staff not usually involved with inventory should supervise the count. Inventory should be tidied and marked to enable counting. Production should be restricted during the count. There should be no inventory movements during the count. Damaged, slow-moving or third party inventory should be isolated so that it can be counted separately.

(b) **Counting**: This should be systematic to ensure that all inventory is counted. Counters should work in pairs with one counting and the other checking the count. There should also be independent checks of counts.

(c) **Recording**: Inventory sheets should be serially numbered to ensure none are omitted or lost. There should be control over the use and return of inventory sheets. Inventory sheets should be completed in ink and signed by the counter. Sufficient information should be recorded on the sheets (inventory item, location, quantity, condition, stage of production). Last goods in and out should be recorded. If inventory records are maintained, the inventory count records should be reconciled with them and any differences investigated.

Attendance at inventory count

At the inventory count, the auditor should carry out planned procedures. This will include:

- Ensuring client staff members are following the inventory count instructions properly
- Making test counts to ensure that procedures are operating effectively
- Obtaining information about damaged or obsolete items and assessing work in progress for its completion
- Confirming that goods that should not be counted (for example, inventories belonging to third parties) have not been included
- Ensuring that inventory movements are minimised and properly accounted for if not
- Obtaining details of last goods in and out of the warehouse for cut off purposes.

The auditor attending the inventory count will be required to conclude whether the inventory count appears to have been properly carried out and whether it provides a suitable basis for determining the existence of inventory.

In addition, the attending auditor should note whether there should be any amendment to planned inventory procedures at the final audit as a result of any matter arising at the count.

After the inventory count

At the final audit, audit staff will follow up relevant matters recorded in working papers from the attendance at the inventory count.

The tests to carry out in relation to existence are:

- Ensuring items that were test counted are included on final inventory sheets
- Ensuring that all count records were included in the final inventory sheets and that every item in inventory sheets is supported by a count record

In addition, if material inventories were retained at third parties, they must obtain confirmations from those parties about the existence and condition of those inventories.

If the company operates a continuous inventory system, the auditors should ensure that test counts have been carried out and that discrepancies between recorded inventory and counted inventory have been amended to what was counted.

> ## Task 4
>
> You have been asked to plan an inventory count attendance at MEM. You have telephoned Ben Swales, who is in charge of the inventory count, and he has sent you a copy of the inventory taking instructions that have been circulated to all staff involved. The count will take place on the year end date, and the factory will not be operating on that day. MEM is not making any deliveries on the day, and is not expecting any deliveries in.
>
> Set out the matters you should consider in planning to attend the inventory count.

The auditors will also carry out additional tests on cut-off and valuation, which we go on to examine now.

CUT OFF OF INVENTORY

Exactly when cut off is critical depends on the nature of the production cycle, but there are four points when it is potentially important. These are when:

- Raw materials are received by the company
- Raw materials are brought from stores into production
- Work-in-progress is taken into finished goods inventories
- Finished goods are despatched to customers

HOW IT WORKS

The key issue is that the company should not count assets twice or fail to record liabilities.

For example, if the company delivers goods to a customer without removing those goods from inventory records and also records the sale, the asset is being counted twice (as inventory and as a receivable), meaning that profit will be overstated (both the sale and the impact of closing inventory are being counted here).

For example, if the company purchases goods from a supplier and counts those goods in inventory but does not record the purchase, the asset is being counted without any corresponding liability being recognised (as it is in inventory, but not in payables), and profit is once again overstated (as closing inventory is inflated, but purchases is not).

At the inventory count

Remember, at the inventory count, the attending auditor should have observed controls over movements of inventory during the count and obtained records of all goods that did move during the count.

The auditor should also have obtained details of the last goods received into the company and the last goods sent out.

Final audit

At the final audit, these details will be followed up to ensure that the inventory records are correct.

The goods received note for the last goods in will be matched with purchase invoices to ensure that it was correctly recorded (as were subsequent purchases).

The goods out note for the last goods out will be matched with sales invoices to ensure that it was correctly recorded (as were subsequent sales).

If there were movements between raw materials, work in progress and finished goods, the auditors would also follow up those movements.

VALUATION OF INVENTORY

You should know the key accounting requirement for inventory, that goods should be valued at the lower of cost and net realisable value.

Raw materials

Raw materials are tested to ensure that they are held at cost. This is because it is extremely unlikely that net realisable value would differ from cost for raw materials, unless they had been damaged or the value was affected by age.

Task 5

Set out why net realisable value is likely to be the same as cost for bought in goods.

First, auditors must understand how the company determines the cost of raw materials.

The company might be able to identify each item separately, in which case, they can be valued at their own original cost.

However, it will not be possible to value some inventory in this way because of the nature of it, and the company will have to use a technique, such as FIFO (first in first out) which you should be aware of.

HOW IT WORKS

Imagine that a company purchases the same goods over and over again and that they are stored in a giant bin. How is the company to know which individual items of inventory were the ones purchased in April and which in May? If the price hasn't changed, this doesn't matter, but if the price has changed over the period in which the inventories could have been purchased, they will need to calculate the best price at which to value all that inventory, although it may all have been bought at different prices.

In a FIFO system, the company would assume that the inventory purchased earliest is also sold earliest (the **first in** is also the **first out**) so that the inventory should be valued at the most recent prices.

The auditors must ensure that the method used to approximate to cost is fair and consistent with prior years.

They will verify prices to purchase invoices or third party evidence such as suppliers' price lists.

Work-in-progress

You should know that accounting standards define 'cost' as 'cost of purchase plus the cost of conversion'.

The cost of conversion becomes relevant when considering work-in-progress and finished goods. It will include:

- Directly attributable costs (for example, labour, machine costs)
- Other production costs (lighting in the factory, for example)

The auditors will need to test the company's calculation of cost of conversion. In general terms, the auditors may apply analytical procedures (for example, comparing similar inventory lines from this year to last year to see if any changes in price appear reasonable). They can also carry out other tests:

- Checking labour costs to wage records
- Checking labour time to production records
- If a standard cost is used, comparing this to actual costs
- Checking other relevant costs (such as electricity) to invoices

The allocation of production overheads must be done on the basis of normal activity, and the auditors must ensure that the overall calculations are reasonable.

Finished goods

Finished goods are most likely to be affected by net realisable value, as there is a market for them. Work in progress might also be affected by net realisable value, but this would be more difficult to judge.

Net realisable value is the estimated or actual selling price of the goods.

Task 6

Set out what factors might increase the likelihood of net realisable value being lower than the cost of the goods.

The auditors should ensure any goods they noted as being obsolete or damaged at the inventory count have been reduced in value. They should also carry out the following tests:

- Examine sales prices after the year end for a sample of goods and compare them to the cost at which the inventories were valued

- Review quantities of inventory items sold after the year end to ensure that inventory is likely to be sold

- Consider whether allowances need to be made for goods that have not moved for a long time and do not appear to be selling after the year end

Task 7

Inventory values at Kingshill Ltd are as follows:

Inventory item	Cost	NRV
Part X	100	200
Part Y	150	100

There are 100 X parts and 100 Y parts on the final inventory sheets. Which of the following options shows the correct value in the financial statements for the two parts?

A   £20,000

B   £25,000

C   £30,000

D   £35,000

CHAPTER OVERVIEW

- Inventory can be difficult to audit because it is often material in total, but comprises a large number of small items

- In addition, the complications of accounting for inventory add to the difficulty in auditing inventory

- Key assertions to test are existence, completeness and valuation

- Key controls to consider are the controls over the counting of inventory to prove its existence

- The auditor should attend an inventory count to obtain sufficient appropriate information about the existence of inventory

- The auditor should obtain inventory-taking instructions and ensure that they seem capable of ensuring an efficient count

- The attending auditor should ensure that inventory count instructions are followed and should carry out test counts to check the count is adequate

- The attending auditor should also obtain details of the last goods in and out of the company prior to the inventory count

- At the final audit, the auditors should follow up inventory count testing and ensure identified goods were included in final inventory sheets

- They should trace the cut-off information to purchase and sales invoices to ensure cut-off was recorded correctly

- They should also test the valuation of inventory, focusing on cost and, where relevant, net realisable value

TEST YOUR LEARNING

Test 1 Select whether the following statements are True or False.

	Options
Inventory is difficult to audit because it often consists of a large number of low value items which are collectively material.	True False
Key assertions to test in relation to inventory are existence, completeness and valuation.	True False

Test 2 Set out why auditors review the inventory counting instructions.

Test 3 Which one of the following best describes what an auditor will do at an inventory count?

Ensure that inventory count procedures are capable of producing an appropriate figure for inventory in the financial statements. ☐

Ensure that inventory count instructions are being followed and some substantive testing, such as observing damaged goods ☐

Ensure that inventory count instructions are being followed and that valuation procedures are appropriate ☐

Certifying that the counts carried out by client staff are correct ☐

Test 4 Select whether the following statements are True or False.

	Options
It is important to record cut off correctly so that assets are not double counted (receivables and inventory).	True False
It is important to record cut off correctly so that a liability is not omitted in respect of an asset (payables and inventory).	True False
For the purposes of the financial statements, it does not matter if the company misstates cut off between raw materials and work-in-progress.	True False

Test 5 The objective of a substantive test will determine the source of evidence obtained. For each of the objectives set out below, select the source of evidence.

	Options
Obtain evidence of the value of raw material.	Purchase invoice Sales invoice Both
Obtain evidence of the value of finished goods.	Purchase invoice Sales invoice Both

Test 6 Complete the following statement about how net realisable value is tested, by filling in the words selected from the pick list below.

Net realisable value is tested with reference to after year-end .... The value of items of inventory is compared to post-year end .... This is to ensure that inventory value is equal to or .... than net realisable value of the inventory.

Pick list

Sales

Purchases

Sales invoices

Purchase invoices

Higher

Lower

Test 7 Here are the inventory taking instructions for the year ended 31 December 20X8 from MEM that Ben Swales passed on to you so that you might plan your audit.

The inventory count will be supervised by Ben Swales and Marie Edgehill. The evening before the inventory count please tidy the area in which you work and ensure that all inventory is where it should be.

There will be no production on 31 December 20X8. You should not move any inventory on that day without permission from Ben Swales. Warehouse staff should provide Ben with the details of the last goods received and sent out from the warehouse.

Each counter should collect a prenumbered inventory count sheet from Ben. He should count the inventory in the area that has been allocated to him and record it on the inventory sheet (giving inventory code, quantity, quality and location) in pen. When inventory has been counted, a blue sticker should be attached to it so that it is not counted twice.

When you have counted all the inventory in your area, return the inventory count sheet to Marie or Ben. You should sign the inventory count sheet to confirm that you have counted everything in your area. Marie or Ben will perform some test counts in your area. Once test counts have been performed, if your count appears to have been completed reasonably, you will be allowed to go home. Do not go home without the express permission of Marie or Ben.

Comment on whether you feel the count is likely to be effective for the purposes of establishing the existence of inventory.

Test 8 Auditors will carry out the following tests when auditing inventory. From the options provided, select which important assertion about inventory that each test is seeking to prove in the first instance.

	Options
Attending an inventory count	Existence
	Completeness
	Valuation
Tracing counted items to final inventory sheets	Existence
	Completeness
	Valuation
Reviewing after year end sales invoices	Existence
	Completeness
	Valuation

Test 9 You have carried out the following work on inventory cut off on the audit of MEM.

Client	MEM		Prepared by	Student
Accounting date	31 December 20X8		Date	6 April 20X9
			Reviewed by	
			Date	

INVENTORY CUT OFF

Last deliveries out (excluded from inventory count?)

Goods out note	Sales order	Customer	Agreed to Dec Sales
27555	19426	Harveys	Yes
27556	19207	Farrows	Yes

Last goods received (included in inventory count?)

GRN	Agreed to invoice?
98854	Yes – purchase invoice number 29444, value £309
	This invoice is included in January purchases

Which one of the following conclusions is most suitable in respect of this test?

Cut-off has been recorded properly. No further tests are required. ☐

Sales cut-off appears to have been recorded properly. Purchases cut-off does not appear to have been recorded properly. Further tests should be carried out on deliveries received before the year end. ☐

Purchases cut-off appears to have been recorded properly. Sales cut-off does not appear to have been recorded properly. Further tests should be carried out on deliveries received before the year end. ☐

Cut-off does not appear to have been recorded properly. Further cut-off tests of both purchases and sales are required. ☐

Test 10 Here is a completed working paper in respect of valuation of inventory at MEM.

Client: MEM	Prepared by: Student
Accounting date: 31 December 20X8	Date: 11 April 20X9
	Reviewed by:
	Date:

Inventory valuation

Item	Quantity	Cost £	Value correct?	Lower than NRV?
E5669356SH	47	0.69	Y	Y
J4622284FR	378	1.47	Y	Y
L3889355OS	34	1.33	Y	Y
Q7669245YJ	604	12.07	Y*	Y
Z8335745DG	444	38.30	Y*	N

*Translated from Euros at yearend exchange rate

Conclusion

The Z8335745s in inventory should be written down to their Net Realisable Value of £36.90.

This will result in the following journal:

Dr Closing inventory in the Statement of Comprehensive Income £622
Cr Inventory in the Statement of Financial Position £622

Select items from the pick list below to indicate which documents the student has referred to in order to complete this test.

(i)   Value correct

....

(ii)   Lower than NRV

....,

Pick list

Inventory sheets

Purchase invoices

20X8 Sales price list

20X9 Sales price list

Minutes of directors' meetings

chapter 8:
AUDIT OF OTHER ASSETS (AND RELATED ITEMS)

── **chapter coverage** 📖 ──

In this chapter I will go through the basic auditing techniques for other major asset categories. I will also touch on the types of tests that auditors carry out on related expenses and income: for example, depreciation, irrecoverable receivable expense and sales. The topics covered are:

✍ Non-current assets

✍ Intangible non-current assets

✍ Prepayments

✍ Sales

✍ Bank and cash

NON-CURRENT ASSETS

NON-CURRENT ASSETS are assets held for continuing use in the business. They are sometimes known as fixed assets.

Introduction to non-current assets

You should know all about non-current assets from your accounting studies. There are several categories of non-current asset (property, plant and equipment, for example). As these are likely to be the major assets a company owns, these might well be material.

Task 1

Using your knowledge of non-current assets, set out what you think the key issues will be for auditors.

The key assertions that auditors will be concerned with are completeness, rights and obligations (ie ownership), existence and valuation. It is important to understand the distinction between ownership and existence in this context. For example, it may be clear to the auditor that a factory exists – particularly if he is working in it. However, if the company does not own that building, it would be wrong to include the value of it in the financial statements.

Auditors are likely to focus on movements in non-current assets in the year (additions and disposals).

Completeness

- Obtain a summary of non-current assets and reconcile with the opening position (additions and disposals)
- Compare non-current assets in the general ledger with the non-current asset register and obtain explanations for any differences
- Check that assets which physically exist are included in the register

Rights and obligations

Land and buildings

- Check title deeds, land registry certificates or leases

Vehicles

- Check registration documents and ensure they are registered in the company name

It is particularly important to check ownerships for new assets in the year. Other documents that indicate title are purchase invoices, architects' certificates, contracts and hire purchase agreements (depending on the nature of the asset).

Existence

All assets

- Inspect assets (focus on additions and high value items) to ensure they exist and are in use and good condition
- Reconcile opening and closing vehicles by number as well as by amount

Valuation

All assets

- Agree value to evidence of cost (if applicable), for example, purchase invoice, contract, lease
- Review depreciation rates for reasonableness (given asset lives, residual values, replacement policy, possible obsolescence)
- Ensure depreciation has been charged appropriately where required
- Recalculate depreciation
- Check disclosure of depreciation rates in the financial statements

Revalued assets

- Verify valuation to the valuation certificate
- Consider reasonableness of valuation – valuer qualified/independent?

Other matters

The auditors will need to consider additions to non-current assets to ensure that each item capitalised does meet the definition of a non-current asset and should not have been expensed as maintenance or repairs or some other expense. In addition, the auditor should review sensitive expense codes such as repairs and maintenance to ensure that they do not include items that should have been capitalised as assets.

Auditors should also test that profits or losses on disposals of assets are calculated properly, verify the disposal proceeds and ensure that the asset has been removed properly from non-current assets.

Task 2

HEC owns the following non-current assets:

- High street shop
- Delivery van
- Shop fittings

Task

Set out, in a manner suitable for inclusion in the audit plan, the audit tests that should be carried out on the above assets to ensure that they are fairly stated in the financial statements. Your summary should include the purpose of each test.

The auditor may also need to consider the treatment of assets which have been constructed by the company rather than purchased (self-constructed assets). In this case, the auditor will need to verify the individual elements of cost. Recommended audit procedures include:

- Verify material and labour costs and overheads to invoices and wage records

- Ensure expenditure has been analysed correctly and properly charged to capital

- Check no profit element has been included in costs

- Check finance costs have been capitalised on a consistent basis

TRADE RECEIVABLES

Introduction to trade receivables

TRADE RECEIVABLES is the amount owed by customers in respect of credit sales.

The key assertions relating to trade receivables that auditors will test are rights and obligations and existence and valuation.

In other words, they will test that the debts are genuinely money owed to the company. They will then assess whether the company is likely to receive the full value of the debt, or whether an allowance needs to be made against the debt.

Existence and rights and obligations

Auditors will obtain details about the receivables' balance from the list of accounts on the sales ledger. They should ensure that this list reconciles to the general ledger and adds up correctly.

The best way to obtain information about the existence of the debts and the company's right to be paid is to seek confirmation from the customers themselves. Therefore, where possible, the auditors will request that the company writes to a sample of receivables to confirm the balances, known as a receivables' circularisation (direct confirmation).

The receivables' circularisation

When circularising receivables the method of requesting information may either be 'positive' or 'negative'.

Under the positive method the customer is asked to reply and confirm whether the stated balance is correct or not. If the customer does not believe that the balance is correct, he should state what he thinks the balance should be.

Under the negative method, the customer is requested to reply only if the amount stated is disputed.

Of the two methods, the positive circularisation is normally the best one to use as it is designed to encourage definite replies from those circularised. However, there may be instances where the negative method could be used, for example where the client has good internal control, with a large number of small accounts.

HOW IT WORKS

The letters should be sent out in the company's name as circularisation is essentially an act of the client, but the letter must request that the reply be sent directly to the auditor. Letters should be sent out at the year-end date.

This is the letter used by MEM Ltd.

METAL EXTRUSIONS MIDLANDS LIMITED
Trading Estate, Maintown

Adams Machines Ltd
123 Long Lane
Brownley

Dear Sir/Madam,

Our auditors, Mason and Co have requested us to ask you to kindly confirm to them directly your indebtedness to us at (insert date) which, according to our records, amounts to £.......... as shown by the enclosed statement.

If the above amount agrees with your records, please sign in the space provided below and post this letter direct to our auditors in the enclosed stamped addressed envelope.

If the amount does not agree with your records, please let our auditors know directly of the amount shown by your records, and if possible, detail on the reverse of this letter full particulars of the difference.

Yours faithfully,

Chief Accountant
Metal Extrusions Midlands Ltd

Balance per sales ledger: £27,354

We agree with this balance ☐

We dispute this balance (give details) ☐

Signed:

Follow-up procedures

Auditors will have to carry out further work in respect of:

- Receivables that disagree with the balance
- Receivables that do not reply

When a debtor disputes the balance, the auditor should seek to reconcile the two balances. The difference may be as a result of timing issues, wrong posting or a dispute, in which case the auditor may need to assess whether the company is genuinely owed the balance.

If receivables do not reply, the auditors should send follow-up requests. However, if the receivables do not reply to the follow-up, there are alternative procedures that auditors need to carry out:

- Check receipts after the year-end date

- Verify purchase orders to see if the debt appears genuine

- Confirm that the debt relates to specific invoices and confirm their validity and that previous items have been paid

- Check if the total is growing and if so, see why (see also valuation of debts below)

Issues connected with the sample

When sampling receivables, it is important that the sample could be chosen from all receivables. You must also consider the following accounts:

- Old unpaid accounts
- Credit balances
- Zero balances
- Accounts which have been paid by the date of examination
- Accounts written-off during the period
- Accounts settled by round sum payment

Valuation of receivables

Testing cash received after date will give evidence that debts were valued correctly.

If cash has not been received after the year-end in respect of debts, this may itself indicate that the debts are not going to be paid and therefore valuation is overstated.

The auditor should carry out the following tests:

- Review sales ledger for old debts which are still unpaid

- Confirm adequacy of any provision made against irrecoverable receivables by reviewing correspondence with receivables and talking to credit controller

- Examine credit notes issued after date to see if they affect the valuation of debts recorded

- Investigate unusual items on the receivables' ledger

Task 3

The auditors do not carry out a circularisation of receivables at HEC, but because receivables tend to pay reasonably promptly, test according to receipts after date instead.

Here is a sample of receivables at the year-end:

	£
Grand Hotel, The	10,593
Happy Eatin'	9,967
Secret Garden	6,898
Quinn's Fine Dining	2,831
Victorine's	1,936

Here are some extracts from the cash book since the year-end:

	£
Jan	
Turners'	311
The Dell	445
The Grand Hotel	4,569
Victorine's	1,936
Happy Eatin'	4,792
Laurels	377
Feb	
The Grand Hotel	6,024
Victorine's	938
Secret Garden	3,892
Happy Eatin'	5,175

Task

Complete the following working paper by inserting the correct amounts and words in the blank boxes below.

Client:	HEC		Prepared by:	Student
Accounting date:	31 December 20X8		Date:	8 April 20X9
			Reviewed by:	
			Date:	

Trade receivables

Receivables	Balance per sales ledger	Receipts after date (Jan)	Receipts after date (Feb)	Reconciled?
Grand Hotel	10,593	4,569	☐	☐
Happy Eatin'	9,967	4,792	5,175	Yes
Secret Garden	☐	–	3,892	☐
Quinn's	2,831	–	–	No
Victorine's	☐	1,936	938*	Yes

* Balance reconciled in January.

Further work required

Victorine's – check that £938 relates to January invoices.

Secret Garden – check whether £3,892 received relates to an invoice or group of invoices and ensure that oldest invoices have been paid. Ensure outstanding balance also relates to an invoice or group of invoices.

Quinns – check how old the balance is and what Quinn's past pattern of payment has been. If it appears the debt may be doubtful, discuss with Peter Tyme to see if action has been taken and whether the debt has been provided against.

If debt appears doubtful and no adjustment has been made, the following journal should be made:

Dr	☐	£2,831
Cr	☐	£2,831

PREPAYMENTS

PREPAYMENTS are assets which arise when a company pays for an expense in advance of receiving the goods or service (eg insurance). They might also arise when a company pays for something annually, but this payment does not coincide with the year-end, meaning that the company has paid for a portion of the item in advance of the financial year to which it relates.

To test prepayments, auditors should:

- Check the payments to the cashbook, expense invoices and correspondence

- Recalculate prepayments

- Review the statement of comprehensive income to ensure that all likely prepayments have been accounted for

- Perform analytical procedures by comparing prepayments with previous years to see if they appear reasonable

SALES

Often, when auditors are auditing receivables, they will audit the related financial statement total of sales (revenue).

Key assertions relating to sales are completeness and accuracy. The auditor wants to confirm that all relevant sales have been included and that sales actually do relate to the correct year. We have considered the issues of cut-off on sales in connection with inventory.

Completeness

Sales are often tested by analytical procedures, as there is usually a great deal of information available in a company about its sales and it should be possible to see predictable relationships arising.

Auditors should:

- Review the level of sales over the year, comparing it on a month-by-month basis with previous years

- Consider the effect that any price rises have had on quantity of sales

- Consider the effect that any price rises or changes in products have had on sales

- Consider the level of goods returned, sales allowances and discounts

In addition, the auditors may test the completeness of recording of sales in the original records, for example, tracing from documents that first record sales right through to the general ledger.

So for example, the auditor may trace through from a sales order to a goods despatch note to an invoice to the sales day book to the sales ledger to the general ledger.

In a cash business, the auditor may trace from the till roll to the sales day book to the sales ledger to the general ledger.

Accuracy

The auditors should also check that sales have been measured correctly by:

- Checking calculations and additions on sales invoices
- Ensuring VAT has been dealt with appropriately
- Checking discounts have been applied properly
- Checking the casting of the sales ledger accounts and control account

Task 4

HEC makes a large number of cash sales. Set out, in a format suitable for inclusion in an audit plan, tests that the auditors should carry out to ensure that sales are completely recorded in the financial statements.

BANK AND CASH

When auditing the client's bank balance, the auditors will be concerned with completeness, existence, rights and obligations and valuation.

All of these assertions can be tested by obtaining confirmation from the client's bank in a device known as a bank letter.

In some businesses, the cash float present on company premises is very small. In others, such as retail operations and hotels, it may be much larger. However, whether cash is material or not, it will often be tested for completeness, as cash balances are highly susceptible to theft.

Bank

The auditor will request confirmation of the client's bank balances in writing from the bank. This request should be made a month before the company's year-end to give the bank a chance to be aware on the correct date. The bank will only respond if they have prior written agreement from the company. Thus, it is important on a first audit to ensure that the company writes to the bank and gives permission well in advance of the year-end.

The letter requests the following information:

- Account and balance details
- Facilities available to the company (for example, overdrafts)
- Any securities given by the company for any loans
- Any other banking relationships

Remember, a company's bank account may be an asset, but it may alternatively be a liability if the company has an overdraft.

It is extremely unlikely that the balance per the company's cashbook will agree with the bank statement and the bank letter on the year-end date. This is commonly due to timing differences of items passing through the bank but not the books or *vice versa*. The company should produce a bank reconciliation every month reconciling the company's position to the bank's position.

The auditors will check the items on this reconciliation to see if they are reasonable. They must watch out for something known as 'window-dressing', where, in order to make the bank balance look more healthy, the company deliberately records purchase payments in the cashbook but does not actually send out cheques, or keeps the cashbook open to record sales receipts actually received after the year-end.

Tests the auditors will carry out:

- Check the arithmetic of the reconciliation

- Agree balances given on reconciliation to the bank letter and cashbook

- Trace outstanding cheques on the reconciliation to after-date bank statements and obtain explanations for items not yet cleared

- Verify that uncleared bankings have cleared by the time of the audit

- Obtain explanations for items in cashbook not in bank statements and *vice versa*

Cash

Auditors may carry out a cash count to ensure that cash floats are fairly stated. Such cash counts should ideally be a surprise.

The auditor should check that the related cashbook is written-up in ink. At no time should the auditor be alone with the cash balance.

After the auditor has counted the cash, it may be necessary to carry out follow-up procedures, for example, to ensure that any 'IOUs' have been reimbursed.

Task 5

In a manner suitable for inclusion in an audit plan, set out the audit work that should be carried out on bank and cash at HEC, giving reasons for each test.

Task 6

The audit team have extracted a list of balances on the sales ledger that were more than 90 days old at the year-end (31 December) and that were still outstanding two months later. The following table gives information relating to these debts.

£24,000 Staceys Ltd	Credit note issued 30 December.
£400 Princes Ltd	Customer takes on average 150 days to pay balance.
£6,000 Gaston Ltd	Cash receipt covering balance in full received 1 March.
£7,500 Ariel Ltd	Credit note issued 24 February.

Which of the following is the value that should be included in the financial statements in respect of these receivables?

A   £400

B   £6,400

C   £13,900

D   £37,900

CHAPTER OVERVIEW

- Auditors will test non-current assets for completeness, existence, rights and obligations and valuation

- Key documents in testing title are title deeds (for property) and registration documents (for vehicles)

- Auditors will focus on movements in the non-current assets balance (that is, additions, disposals and depreciation)

- Auditors will test trade receivables for existence, rights and obligations and valuation

- Existence and rights will be tested by circularising receivables

- Valuation is tested by looking at payments after-date

- Prepayments are tested by looking at cash payments and checking the calculations of the prepayments

- Sales are commonly tested by analytical procedures, but may also be tested by tracing sales transactions through the system from original documents to ensure complete recording

- Bank balances are tested for completeness, existence, rights and obligations and valuation

- All of these can be tested by obtaining a bank letter confirming the bank balance and carrying out tests on the client's reconciliation between bank records and the cashbook

- Cash balances are often counted to test completeness, even if they are immaterial to the statement of financial position

Keywords

Non-current assets – assets held for continuing use in the business

Trade receivables – the amount owed by customers in respect of credit sales

Prepayments – assets which arise when a company pays for an expense in advance of receiving the goods or service

TEST YOUR LEARNING

Test 1 Which of the following statements best summarises the assertions auditors are concerned with in respect of non-current assets?

– Auditors are concerned with completeness, existence, rights and obligations and valuation

– Auditors are concerned with completeness, existence and valuation

– Auditors are concerned with existence, valuation and occurrence

– Auditors are concerned with existence, valuation, occurrence and accuracy

Test 2 Complete the following statements concerning key controls over non-current assets, by filling in the gaps using the items in the pick list below.

A key control is the non-current asset ...., in which every asset should be recorded. Additionally, the company should ensure that additions and disposals are properly ....

Pick list

Authorised

Managed

Register

Account code

Test 3 Auditors usually test receivables by carrying out a circularisation and/or review receipts after the year-end. Using the options provided below, select which assertions the auditors are seeking evidence about.

	Options
Receivables circularisation	Rights and obligations Valuation Both
Reviewing sales and receipts after year-end	Rights and obligations Valuation Both

Test 4 State whether the following statements are True or False in respect of the receivables circularisation.

	Options
The receivables circularisation is sent out in the audit firm's name.	True
	False
Zero balances should not be included in the receivables circularisation.	True
	False
The positive form of circularisation, where customers are asked to reply whether they agree the balance or not is the better form of receivables circularisation.	True
	False

Test 5 Which of the following statements concerning the audit of sales is incorrect?

– Auditors usually rely 100% of controls over sales by carrying out only controls testing.

– Auditors may test controls over sales but will also carry out some substantive tests, often restricted to analytical procedures as there is usually ample evidence concerning a company's sales.

– Auditors will often only test sales by analytical procedures as there is usually ample evidence concerning a company's sales.

– Auditors will sometimes test completeness of sales by tracing a sample of sales from order to general ledger.

Test 6

	Options
Bank letter requests are sent out by the auditor directly to the bank.	True
	False
Bank letter requests should be made at the year-end date.	True
	False
Auditors will commonly test cash balances even if they are not material.	True
	False

Test 7 Here is a schedule of additions to non-current assets at MEM.

	£
Extruding machine X01	20,000
Cutting machine C0425	5,995
Computer	595
Filing cabinet	20

Materiality has been set at £5,000.

Task

In a manner suitable for inclusion in an audit plan, set out the tests that should be carried out in respect of existence, rights and obligations and valuation of non-current asset additions at MEM, commenting on the sample to be selected.

Test 8 Below is a working paper setting out the audit work done in relation to the receivables circularisation for MEM.

Client: MEM			Prepared by:	Student
Accounting date: 31 December 20X8			Date:	9 April 20X9
			Reviewed by:	
			Date:	

Customer	Balance per ledger £	Reply received?	Balance agreed?	Reconciling items
Adams	27,354	Y	Y	N/A
Caterham	38,094	Y	N	Credit note £170 agreed
Dennings	46,299	N	–	
Eastern	323	Y	Y	
Fowlers	10,910	Y	Y	
Gunners	2,488	Y	Y	
Kellers	50,829	Y	N	Credit note £7,325 agreed – damaged goods Receipt £5,711 o/s
Mardons	36,592	Y	Y	
Murphys	4,588	Y	Y	
Petersham	982	Y	Y	
Timmins	3,601	N	–	
Walshes	12,933	Y	Y	

Further work required

Set out the further work required to conclude that trade receivables represent debt genuinely owed to MEM.

Test 9 Here is the bank reconciliation for December 20X8 at MEM.

Bank reconciliation for December 20X8		£
Balance per bank statement:		"21,946
Cheques:	XX0395√	(395)
	XX0396√	(2,644)
	XX0397√	(4,766)
	XX0398√	(477)
	XX0399√	(2,392)
	XX0400√	(911)
	XX0401√	(12)
	XX0402√	(5,783)
	XX0403√	(14,922)
Payments in:	2044×	12,944
	2045×	3,928
	2046×	322
Balance per cash book:		6,838

Audit key ^

^ = Adds correctly
" = Agreed to ....
√ = Agreed to ....
× = Agreed to ....

Using the pick list, complete the audit key showing where items have been verified to in order to audit the bank reconciliation.

Pick list

Bank statement

Bank letter

Bank statements after the year-end date

Cash book after the year-end date

Bank statements prior to the year-end date

Cash book after the year-end date

chapter 9:
AUDIT OF LIABILITIES (AND RELATED ITEMS)

---

chapter coverage 📖

In this chapter I will go through the basic auditing techniques for the major liability categories and the types of tests that auditors carry out on related expense items (for example, purchases or payroll). The topics covered are:

✍ Trade payables

✍ Purchases

✍ Accruals

✍ Payroll

✍ Non current liabilities

✍ Accounting estimates

✍ Other items

TRADE PAYABLES

TRADE PAYABLES is amounts the company owes to its suppliers (also known as trade creditors).

Introduction to trade payables

The key assertion relating to trade payables (and creditors generally) is **completeness**. Auditors should always be aware that a company might want to **understate** its creditors.

Other related assertions are existence and rights and obligations.

Completeness, existence and rights and obligations

When auditing trade payables, the auditors' starting point is the balances on the purchase ledger. The auditor should ensure that the purchase ledger casts correctly and reconciles to the purchase ledger control account.

The best test to prove the existence and completeness of payables and the company's obligations to them is to reconcile purchase ledger balances with **supplier statements**.

SUPPLIER STATEMENTS are records of debt sent by the supplier to the company as part of the routine information system.

Because suppliers often send statements to their customers as part of their routine information system, auditors will not usually need to circularise payables in the same way that they circularise receivables.

Task 1

Which one of the following statements is correct?

- Supplier statements are likely to provide good information for the auditors as they cannot be tampered with by the client. ☐

- Supplier statements are likely to provide good information for the auditors as they are generated by a third party. ☐

- Supplier statements are likely to provide good information for the auditors as they have been requested by the auditor. ☐

- Supplier statements are good evidence, but it is usually better to circularise suppliers. ☐

Auditors should compare supplier statements to purchase ledger balances and reconcile any differences.

Sample issues

As auditors are testing for understatement, only selecting the payables with the largest balances at the year-end will not be sensible sample selection. The auditor should select material balances nonetheless. However, when selecting the rest of the sample, the auditor should use judgement and incorporate low and nil balances into the sample as well as higher balances.

Problems with supplier statements

It will not always be possible to test supplier statements as the company may not retain them, or suppliers may not send them in the first place. Additionally, the internal control over purchases may be very weak, or the auditors may have suspicions that payables have been understated and they are not being granted access to the supplier statements.

In situations such as these, the auditors may take the rare step of circularising payables in the same way as they have circularised receivables.

Alternatively, the purchase invoice is also third party evidence. However, given that it is in the possession of the company, its value in terms of evidence is reduced in that it can be manipulated by the company. For example, invoices could be hidden to understate payables if the company wanted. However, the auditor can make use of purchase invoices to verify payables in some circumstances, if the evidence is backed up by analytical evidence, such as typical number of invoices a month as well.

Task 2

Below is a partially completed working paper relating to trade payables at HEC and a number of supplier statements that Rosemary retained at the year-end for the auditors.

Task

Complete the working paper from the information available below, and set out the further work to be done to conclude whether trade payables are fairly stated.

Client:	MEM		Prepared by:	Student
Accounting date:	31 December 20X8		Date:	9 April 20X9
			Reviewed by:	
			Date:	

Trade payables

Supplier	Balance per purchase ledger £	Balance per supplier statement £	Balance agreed	Comments
Applewoods	10,473			
Brilliant Butchers Limited	3,793			
Deepa's Delicacies Limited	587			
Hot Chocolate Limited	34			
Keil Farm Organics	9,572			
Ordinary Organics Limited	392			
Peterwoods Farm Limited	493			
Steepdale Farm	3,947			
Taylors' Farm Produce Limited	8,351			
Very Nice Food Limited	277			

Further work required

APPLEWOODS ORGANIC FARM LIMITED

Amount due from The Heavenly Eating Company Limited:	£10,473

Representing the following invoices:

S13655	£2,583
S13656	£3,857
S13657	£1,294
S13658	£2,739

Brilliant Butchers Limited
December account (HEC Ltd)

	£
1034	477
1035	512
1036	397
1037	468
1038	447
1039	499
1040	384
1041	609
Total	3,793

Deepa's Delicacies Limited

Amount owed by Heavenly Eating Company @ 31.12.20X8	£587

KEIL FARM ORGANICS LIMITED

Statement of account at 31 December 20X8:
Heavenly Eating Company

	£
SI10011	3,592
SI10012	3,029
SI10013	2,951
SI10014	3,418
Total	12,990

Ordinary Organics Limited

Amount owed by HEC Limited at 31 December 20X8	£392

STEEPDALE FARM

Heavenly Eating Company Limited

	£
Invoice 24377	1,211
Invoice 24378	968
Invoice 24379	1,019
Invoice 24380	749
Total	3,947

TAYLORS' FARM PRODUCE LIMITED
HEC – statement of account @ 31 December 20X8

	£
4966	1,593
4967	938
4968	1,320
4969	1,298
4970	920
4971	1,739
4972	543
Total	8,351

PURCHASES

When testing purchases, auditors are concerned with whether they have occurred, whether they are measured correctly, and whether they have been made for valid business reasons.

We have already considered the issue of cut-off on purchases in relation to inventory.

Occurrence

The auditors often test purchases by using analytical procedures.

Auditors should:

- Consider the level of purchases on a month-by-month basis compared with previous years

- Consider the effect on value of purchases of price changes

- Consider the effect on value of purchases of changes in products purchased

- Compare the ratio of trade payables to purchases with previous years

- Compare the ratio of trade payables to inventory with previous years

- Consider the level of major expenses other than purchases in comparison with previous years

In addition, the auditors may test the completeness of recording of purchases in the original records, for example, tracing documents that first record purchases right through to the general ledger.

Also, to check the validity of purchases in the records, the auditors may test individual items in the nominal ledger back through the records to the original purchase order and requisition.

ACCRUALS

ACCRUALS are liabilities other than trade payables that arise when a company has received a benefit which it has not yet paid for. A common example is a wages and salaries creditor which arises at the year-end because wages are often paid in arrears, that is, the employees do the work and then are paid afterwards.

Accruals will often be tested by analytical procedures and auditors will use their knowledge of the business to know whether it is likely that any accruals will arise. The following tests of detail can also be carried out:

- Recalculate accruals

- Verify accruals by reference to subsequent payments

- Review statement of comprehensive income and prior years to consider whether other accruals are required

- Review payments made and invoices received after the year-end to ascertain whether they should have been accrued.

The calculation of some accruals will be straightforward. For example, an accrual for PAYE should usually represent one month's deductions from the payroll. This can be easily verified. Similarly, a VAT accrual can be verified to the next VAT return.

PAYROLL

When the auditors are scrutinising payroll-related payables, they may also carry out substantive tests on payroll expense, which is highly likely to be material to the financial statements.

A great deal of testing may be done by analytical procedures, as there are a number of predictable relationships (number of staff, standard rates of pay, ratio of deductions to pay etc).

However, the auditor may also carry out tests of detail in relation to occurrence, measurement and completeness.

Occurrence

- Check individual remuneration per payroll to personnel records
- Confirm existence of employees by meeting them
- Check benefits to supporting documentation

Accuracy

- Recalculate benefits
- Check whether deductions of tax and NI have been made correctly
- Check validity of other deductions, eg pension contributions to conditions of pension scheme

Completeness

- Check a sample of employees from records to the payroll
- Check whether joiners have been paid in the correct month
- Check whether leavers have been correctly removed from payroll
- Check casts of the payroll
- Confirm payment of pay to bank transfer records
- Agree net pay per cashbook to payroll
- Scrutinise payroll and investigate unusual items

NON CURRENT LIABILITIES

NON CURRENT LIABILITIES are loans repayable at a date more than one year after the year-end. Examples include bank loans and debentures.

Introduction to non current liabilities

Auditors are concerned with completeness, valuation and disclosure.

Completeness

- Obtain/prepare a schedule of loans outstanding at the end of the reporting period
- Compare opening balances to the previous year's working papers (closing balances at the end of last year)
- Test the clerical accuracy of the schedule
- Compare balances to the general ledger
- Check the names of lenders to relevant information (such as bank letter or register of debenture-holders)
- Review minutes and cashbook to ensure that all loans have been recorded

Valuation

- Trace additions and repayments to entries in the cashbook

- Confirm repayments are in accordance with the loan agreement

- Examine receipts for loan repayments

- Obtain direct confirmation from lenders about amounts loaned and the terms thereof

- Verify interest charged for the period and the adequacy of accrued interest

Disclosure

Review the disclosures made in the financial statements and ensure they meet legal requirements

---

Task 3

You have noted on the bank letter that HEC has a mortgage which is repayable over 20 years. Set out, in a format suitable for inclusion in an audit plan, the audit procedures to be carried out on this loan.

ACCOUNTING ESTIMATES

An ACCOUNTING ESTIMATE is an approximation of the amount of an item in the absence of a precise means of measurement. Examples include:

- Allowances to reduce inventories and receivables to their estimated realisable value

- Depreciation

- Accrued revenue

- Provision for a loss from a lawsuit

- Provision to meet warranty claims

Directors and management are responsible for making accounting estimates included in the financial statements. These estimates are often made in conditions of **uncertainty** regarding the outcome of events and involve the use of judgement. The risk of a material misstatement therefore increases when accounting estimates are involved (and thus inherent risk is higher). **Audit evidence** supporting accounting estimates is generally less than conclusive and so auditors need to exercise **significant judgement**.

Accounting estimates may be produced as part of the routine operations of the accounting system, or may be a non-routine procedure at the period end.

Where, as is frequently the case, a **formula** based on past experience is used to calculate the estimate, it should be reviewed regularly by management (for example, actual v estimate in prior periods).

Audit procedures

The auditors should gain an understanding of the procedures and methods used by management to make accounting estimates. This will aid the auditors' planning of their own procedures. Auditors must carry out one or a mixture of the following procedures.

Procedure 1 – Review and testing the process

The auditors should:

- Evaluate the data and consider the assumptions on which the estimate is based

- Test the calculations involved in the estimate

- Compare estimates made for prior periods with actual results of those periods

- Consider management's/directors' review and approval procedures

Procedure 2 – Use of an independent estimate

Such an estimate (made or obtained by the auditors) may be compared with the accounting estimate.

Procedure 3 – Review of subsequent events

The auditors should review transactions or events after the period-end which may reduce or even remove the need to test accounting estimates. For example, if directors have estimated a allowance for an irrecoverable receivable, but all debt existing at the end of the reporting period has been paid by the date of the audit report, this provision will no longer be required.

OTHER ITEMS

Share capital, reserves and statutory books are often bracketed together for audit purposes.

The audit objectives are to ascertain that:

- Share capital has been properly classified and disclosed in the financial statements and changes properly authorised.

- Movements on reserves have been properly authorised and, in the case of statutory reserves, only used for permitted purposes.

- Statutory records have been properly maintained and returns properly and expeditiously dealt with.

The auditor is also concerned that Companies Act requirements have been met in terms of disclosures of capital items and director-related disclosures, such as directors' emoluments.

Task 4

The audit junior has completed her audit work reconciling a sample of payables to supplier statements. The following is her reconciliation of the debt owed to Dayglo:

	£	
Balance per supplier:	60,000	
Payment 31 December	(10,000)	Agreed to bank statement 4 January.
Credit note requested	(5,000)	Credit note issued February re December invoice
Balance per ledger	45,000	

Which of the following balances should be included in the financial statements in respect of Dayglo's balance?

A   60,000

B   55,000

C   50,000

D   45,000

CHAPTER OVERVIEW

- Auditors will test trade payables for understatement. They are concerned with existence, obligations and completeness

- Key documents in testing trade payables are supplier statements, which give third party evidence of the liability

- Purchases are often tested by analytical procedures, but can also be subject to tests of detail

- Accruals are also tested by analytical procedures

- The calculation of some accruals will be straightforward and there is good evidence that they are correct (for example, PAYE accrual or VAT accrual)

- When testing payroll-related liabilities, the auditors may also test the payroll expense, which is likely to be a material figure

- Tests of detail are carried out on the payroll to test occurrence, measurement and completeness

- Non current liabilities should be tested for completeness, measurement and disclosure

- Common long-term loans are bank loans (which can be verified with reference to the bank letter) and debentures (which should have legal documentation attached to verify them to)

- The main concern for the auditor in relation to share capital, reserves and directors' emoluments is whether the company has complied with the Companies Act

Keywords

Trade payables – amounts the company owes to its suppliers

Supplier statements – records of debt sent by the supplier to the company as part of the routine information system

Accruals – liabilities other than trade payables that arise when a company has received a benefit which it has not yet paid for

Non current liabilities – loans repayable at a date more than one year after the year-end

Accounting estimate – an approximation of the amount of an item in the absence of a precise means of measurement

TEST YOUR LEARNING

Test 1 Which of the following statements best summarises the assertions auditors are concerned with in respect of trade payables?

- Auditors are concerned with completeness, existence and valuation. ☐

- Auditors are concerned with completeness, existence and obligations. ☐

- Auditors are concerned with existence, obligations and occurrence. ☐

- Auditors are concerned with existence, obligations, occurrence and accuracy. ☐

Test 2 State whether the following statements are True or False in respect of supplier statements.

	Options
They represent a better source of evidence than replies to a receivables circularisation as they are sent direct to the company.	True False
They are only used when the auditor is unable to do a payables circularisation.	True False
Testing supplier statements provides evidence that trade payables have not been understated.	True False

Test 3 Using the pick list below, insert appropriate words to complete the following statements about selecting a sample of trade payables.

Auditors should consider that payables might be .... and therefore not simply select large balances to test (although they must select .... items). .... balances should also be incorporated into the test.

Pick list

Overstated

Understated

Significant

Material

Nil

Test 4 Complete the following definitions by filling in the gaps using the pick list below.

.... are liabilities other than .... that arise because the company has received a benefit it has not yet paid for.

.... are loans repayable at a date .... one year after the year-end.

Pick list

Non current liabilities

Accruals

Other payables

Trade payables

More than

Less than

Equal to

Test 5 Which of the following statements best summarises the assertions auditors are concerned with in respect of payroll expense?

–   Auditors are concerned with completeness, existence and valuation. □

–   Auditors are concerned with completeness, existence and obligations. □

–   Auditors are concerned with occurrence, accuracy and completeness. □

–   Auditors are concerned with obligations, occurrence and completeness. □

Test 6 Below is a partially completed working paper in relation to trade payables at MEM and a selection of supplier statements and other items where supplier statements are not available.

Task

Complete the working paper and draw a conclusion on the test.

Client: MEM		Prepared by:	Student
Accounting date: 31 December 20X8		Date:	10 April 20X9
		Reviewed by:	
		Date:	

Trade payables

Payables	Balance per purchase ledger £	Balance per supplier statement £	Balance agreed	Comments
Calais	156,498			
Denby	3,926			
John Johns	35,792			
Millars	20,692			
Wyndhams	2,967			

Further work required

Calais Métal SARL
60 Rue do la Industrie
Calais

To: Metal Extrusions Midlands Ltd
Trading Estate, Maintown

Equitibre de compte @ 31.12.X8	164,322.90
Factures/invoices: 11249	43,712.69
11254	58,187.50
11275	32,230.11
11276	30,192.60
	164,322.90

The exchange rate at the year-end was £1:1.05€.

DENBY FAMILY COMPANY LTD

8 North Industrial Estate

Large Town

Metal Extrusions Midlands Limited

	£
Balance @ 31.12.X8	**3,926**

Comprising one invoice, invoice number S1297

	John Johns Ltd
	7, Carmichael Way
	Luton
Metal Extrusions Midlands Limited	
Trading Estate	
Maintown	
Invoices outstanding at 31 December 20X8:	
	£
13079	7,954.40
13080	3,244.57
13081	4,725.24
13082	5,954.17
13083	2,891.99
13084	8,349.27
13085	7,327.64
	40,447.28

MILLARS METALS LTD

To: Metal Extrusions Midlands Limited

Trading Estate

Maintown

Invoices outstanding at 31 December 20X8:

	£
2341109	4,721.39
2341111	976.97
2341202	2,174.51
2341271	3,212.74
2341399	1,574.91
2341549	872.90
2341557	1,632.87
2341558	1,714.14
2341559	3,811.49
	20,691.92

WYNDHAMS LIMITED   To: Metal   Extrusions   Midlands Ltd

The Windmill   Trading Estate

Carville   Maintown

Exshire

Invoice no: X22197

Date: 12 December 20X8

		£
W8412669BD	325 × £2.85	926.25
W993673SD	5 × £408.15	2,040.75
		2,967.00

Test 7 Here are two analyses of purchases month-by-month for the last two years at MEM.

	Jan	Feb	Mar	Apr	May	June
	£'000	£'000	£'000	£'000	£'000	£'000
20X7	1,029	989	1,201	1,033	970	1,109
20X8	793	1,195	1,233	1,284	1,302	1,299

	July	Aug	Sept	Oct	Nov	Dec
	£'000	£'000	£'000	£'000	£'000	£'000
20X7	1,097	999	1,021	1,057	1,193	1,540
20X8	1,334	1,465	1,354	1,378	1,399	1,402

Task

Review the two analyses and draw conclusions about whether purchases are fairly stated.

Test 8 Set out the types of accruals you would expect to exist at MEM and the audit work that should be carried out on each.

chapter 10:
AUDIT COMPLETION AND REPORTING

chapter coverage 📖

In this chapter I will summarise other things an auditor must consider before an audit opinion can be given. This includes matters such as whether the company is likely to continue to function, issues that have arisen since the year-end and the overall state of the financial statements. Auditors also take steps to formalise some of the information directors have given them as part of the audit as written representations rather than just oral explanations.

Last, we look at the professional requirements related to reporting, which is, of course, the object of the exercise. The major point of an audit, as you know, is to report on the truth and fairness of the financial statements in the formal auditor's report. However, the auditor is also given a number of other reporting requirements by professional standards. The topics covered are:

✎ Audit completion

✎ Audit reporting

AUDIT COMPLETION

Once auditors have obtained evidence about the individual transactions and balances in the financial statements, there are still a number of things that they are required by professional standards to consider before they can give an opinion on financial statements.

Overall review

The auditor is required to draw an overall conclusion as to whether the financial statements as a whole are consistent with the auditor's understanding of the entity.

Task 1

Set out what auditing technique will be helpful in carrying out this task and how will it be used.

Matters the auditor should consider:

- Whether the financial statements reflect the information and explanations the auditors have been given during the audit

- Whether audit procedures have identified any new factors that will affect the presentation of the financial statements

- Whether analytical procedures (which must be carried out at this stage of the audit) indicate that the financial statements are consistent with themselves

- Whether the presentation of the financial statements has been unduly influenced by the desire of the directors to show the results in a particular way

ISA 700 *Forming an Opinion and Reporting on Financial Statements* also requires auditors to evaluate whether the financial statements are prepared in accordance with the applicable financial reporting framework, which will involve consideration of whether the:

- Accounting policies are appropriate/disclosed adequately

- Accounting estimates used are reasonable

- Information presented in the financial statements is relevant, reliable, comparable and understandable

- Disclosures are adequate

- Terminology used is appropriate

Identified misstatements

As noted in Chapter 5, the auditors maintain a record of all identified misstatements (except those that are clearly trivial). As part of completion procedures, the auditor must evaluate the effect of these identified misstatements on the audit and the effect of uncorrected misstatements on the financial statements.

ISA 450 *Evaluation of Misstatements Identified During the Audit* gives guidance about this.

The auditor must consider if the audit strategy and plan need revision if:

- The nature and circumstances of identified misstatements indicate that other unidentified misstatements exist, the combined total of which might be material.

- The aggregate of identified misstatements approaches the materiality level set by the auditors during planning.

The auditors must make management aware of identified misstatements and request that they are adjusted. If they refuse, the auditors should take their reasons into account when evaluating if the financial statements as a whole are free from material misstatement.

Before assessing the effect uncorrected misstatements have on the financial statements, the auditors should re-confirm that the materiality level remains appropriate. They should then determine whether the aggregate of the uncorrected misstatements is material.

The auditors should communicate the uncorrected misstatements to those charged with governance (listed individually). They should obtain a written representation from management and where appropriate from those charged with governance whether they believe the uncorrected misstatements to be immaterial.

In addition to the list of uncorrected misstatements, the auditors should document the level below which items will be considered trivial and the auditor's conclusion as to whether uncorrected misstatements are material, and the reasons for that conclusion.

Subsequent events

The auditors have to consider matters that have happened since the year-end (subsequent events) and decide whether they affect whether a true and fair view is given. The auditors have already used information from the period after the year end date to ascertain whether a true and fair view is given of assets and liabilities, but they also carry out a formal review.

Task 2

Give three examples of how auditors have used information from the period after the year-end to ascertain whether the financial statements give a true and fair view.

The auditors are required to consider the effect of subsequent events on the financial statements and whether any require adjustments or disclosures to be made in the financial statements.

As part of their risk assessment, the auditors should have considered the procedures that management has in place to determine whether events after the end of the reporting period impact the financial statements.

Examples of matters which might impact the financial statements:

- Outcome of litigation (could affect provisions, liabilities, going concern)
- New commitments or borrowings (might require disclosure)
- New shares or debentures being issued (might require disclosure)

Up to the date of the auditor's report

The auditor is responsible for identifying relevant issues up to the date when the auditor's report is signed, and for ensuring that the directors make relevant adjustments in order for the auditors to conclude a true and fair view is given. They do this by making enquiries of management, and by carrying out other procedures, such as reading minutes of management meetings after the year-end.

After the date of the auditor's report

After the date of the auditor's report, the auditors have a duty to respond appropriately to facts that become known to them. They have no obligation to perform any audit procedures to discover relevant subsequent events after this time. However, if they become aware of issues, they should discuss the matter with management and seek to ensure that shareholders are given appropriate information.

Provisions and contingencies

Sometimes, there are matters outstanding at the year end which could impact on the financial statements were their outcome known. The auditor must ensure that the directors have addressed these matters as required by accounting standards, and either made provision or disclosed matters where relevant.

The audit tests that should be carried out on provisions and contingent assets and liabilities are:

- Obtain details of all provisions which have been included in the accounts and all contingencies that have been disclosed

- Obtain a detailed analysis of all provisions showing opening balances, movements and closing balances

- Determine for each material provision whether the company has a present obligation as a result of past events by:

    - Review of correspondence relating to the item

    - Discussion with the directors. Have they created a valid expectation in other parties that they will discharge the obligation?

- Determine for each material provision whether it is probable that a transfer of economic benefits will be required to settle the obligation by the following tests:

    - Check whether any payments have been made after the period end in respect of the item

    - Review of correspondence with solicitors, banks, customers, insurance company and suppliers both pre- and post-year-end

    - Send a letter to the solicitor to obtain their views (where relevant)

    - Discuss the position of similar past provisions with the directors, were these provisions eventually settled?

    - Consider the likelihood of reimbursement

- Recalculate all provisions made

- Compare the amount provided with any post-year-end payments and with any amount paid in the past for similar items

- In the event that it is not possible to estimate the amount of the provision, check that this contingent liability is disclosed in the accounts

- Consider the nature of the client's business; would you expect to see any other provisions, eg warranties?

Going concern

Another important issue is whether the company will continue to exist. This affects the whole basis of how the financial statements have been put together.

HOW IT WORKS

Take the assertion of valuation, for example. If a company is not going to continue to exist in the foreseeable future, then valuation of assets may well be different than if it were to continue trading.

Usually, assets such as, a factory and machinery are valued at their value to the business, which is depreciated cost. If the company were to cease to exist, they would probably be sold, and so should be valued at market value, which is likely to be different.

If the company is likely to exist in the foreseeable future, it is called a going concern. Most companies are going concerns and the financial statements reflect that. In rare circumstances, usually if the company is in trading difficulties, the directors and auditors may acknowledge that the company is no longer a going concern and will have to be wound-up, in which case, the financial statements would have to be drawn up on a different basis.

When putting together the financial statements, the directors are required to consider whether the company is a going concern.

Accounting standards require the directors to make certain disclosures in respect of going concern:

- Any material uncertainties which cast significant doubt on the entity's ability to continue as a going concern.

- When the directors have only been able to assess a short period into the future (less than one year) in determining whether the company is a going concern.

- When the financial statements are not prepared on a going concern basis. They should then also disclose the basis under which the financial statements are prepared.

The auditors are required to consider the appropriateness of the assumptions made by management and also any disclosures that they have made.

This is a matter that will have been considered throughout the audit. If there was a risk that the company was not a going concern, it is likely that this would have been identified as part of risk assessment procedures.

Task 3

Set out factors which might indicate that a company is not a going concern.

Further audit procedures, usually undertaken when going concern is in doubt, are beyond the scope of your assessment guidance.

Written representations

Auditors will request that management confirms it has fulfilled its responsibilities for the preparation of the financial statements and completeness of information given to the auditors in written representations. They may also request written representations to provide supporting evidence about material matters. Written representations therefore cover:

- Management has fulfilled its responsibility for the preparation of the financial statements and their approval

- Material matters when the auditor believes they are required to support other evidence obtained

- Management's acknowledgement that is has provided the auditor with all relevant information and explanations and that all transactions have been recorded/reflected in the financial statements

When the auditors receive this type of representation they should:

- Evaluate whether the representation appears reasonable and is consistent with other evidence obtained

- Consider whether the individuals making the representations would be expected to be well-informed about the issue

Written representations are limited to those matters that are considered material to the financial statements.

If management refuse to give written representation that it has fulfilled its responsibilities for the financial statements, the auditor would have to give a disclaimer of opinion due to an inability to obtain sufficient appropriate audit evidence (see below).

Completion

The final stage of the audit is very important as it is now that all the evidence is weighed up and a decision is made about whether the auditor can form his audit opinion. The following procedures are normally involved in this process.

- A report to the partner will be produced. This will point the partner in the direction of key issues arising.

- A completion checklist may be used to ensure that all final procedures have been carried out and signed off.

AUDIT REPORTING

The reports that the auditor produces are ultimately the point of the audit.

The most important report is the statutorily required auditor's report. Professional standards set out what this report is required to contain. You were shown an example in Chapter 2. You should refer back to this now.

The auditor may be required under professional standards to issue a number of other reports to management or other parties. We have already looked at the issue of the report on control deficiency in Chapter 4. Reporting relating to fraud is an important issue, and we briefly look at it at the end of this chapter.

Auditor's report

The statutory audit opinion

Auditors are required by the Companies Act to state explicitly whether in their opinion the annual accounts give a true and fair view and whether they have been properly prepared in accordance with the Companies Act and the applicable financial reporting framework (UK GAAP). (We looked at the meaning of 'true and fair' in Chapter 2.)

The auditors must also express an opinion on whether the information given in the directors' report is consistent with the accounts.

In addition, certain requirements are reported on by exception. This means that the auditor only has to report if they have not been met. These are that:

- Adequate accounting records have been kept and proper returns adequate for the audit have been received from branches not visited
- The financial statements are in agreement with the accounting records and returns
- All information and explanations have been received as the auditors think necessary and they have had access at all times to the company's books, accounts and vouchers
- Details of directors' emoluments and other benefits have been correctly disclosed in the financial statements
- Particulars of loans and other transactions in favour of directors and others have been correctly disclosed in the financial statements

The Standard report

The auditing standard relating to auditor's reports requires that an auditor's report display the following elements:

- A title, identifying to whom the report is addressed
- Addressee (normally the shareholders)
- An introductory paragraph identifying the financial statements audited

- A statement of management's responsibility for the financial statements
- A statement of the auditor's responsibility
- Opinion paragraph

Other reporting responsibilities

- The date of the auditor's report
- Auditor's address
- The signature of the auditors

Task 4

Go back to Chapter 2 and find the sample auditor's report given there. Identify the required elements of an auditor's report given above and read carefully through the wording of each one.

Unqualified opinion

If the auditors conclude that the financial statements are prepared in all material respects in accordance with the applicable financial reporting framework, then they will give what is called an unqualified opinion. The example given in Chapter 2 shows an unqualified opinion.

Modified reports

A modified report is issued when the auditors cannot state without reservation that the financial statements are free from material misstatement.

Modified opinions

The auditors will give a modified opinion if:

- They believe the financial statements as a whole, or a material aspect of the financial statements, do not give a true and fair view or contain a material misstatement. This is normally due to a disagreement with management regarding the acceptability of the accounting policies selected, how they have been applied or the adequacy of disclosures

- There has been a limitation on the scope of the audit which does not allow them to draw a conclusion on the financial statements as a whole or on an aspect of them, as sufficient appropriate audit evidence is not available. For example, the timing of the auditor's appointment was such that the auditor was unable to attend the inventory count

HOW IT WORKS

In summary, then, there are four situations in which auditors may give a modified opinion under ISA 705 *Modifications to the Opinion in the Independent Auditor's Report*:

(1) A material aspect of the financial statements is not prepared in accordance with the applicable financial reporting framework but this is not pervasive to the financial statements. In this case, the auditors would give an qualified opinion, stating that everything except the material item is fairly stated. Here is an example of such a qualified opinion:

> **Qualified opinion arising from disagreement about accounting treatment**
>
> **Basis for qualified opinion on financial statements**
>
> Included in the receivables shown on the balance sheet is an amount of £Y due from a company which has ceased trading. XYZ Ltd has no security for this debt. In our opinion, the company is unlikely to receive any payment and full provision of £Y should have been made. Accordingly, debtors should be reduced by £Y, the deferred tax liability should be reduced by £X and profit for the year and retained earnings should be reduced by £Z.
>
> **Qualified opinion on financial statements**
>
> In our opinion, except for the effects of to the matter described in the basis for qualified opinion paragraph, in our opinion the financial statements:
>
> - Give a true and fair view of the state of the company's affairs as at ..... and of its profit (loss) for the year then ended;
>
> - Have been properly prepared in accordance with United Kingdom Generally Accepted Accounting Practice; and
>
> - Have been prepared in accordance with the Companies Act 2006;
>
> **Opinion on other matter prescribed by the Companies Act 2006**
>
> In our opinion the information given in the directors' report for the financial year for which the financial statements are prepared is consistent with the financial statements.
>
> **Matters on which we are required to report by exception**
>
> [unchanged]

(2) The financial statements as a whole do not give a true and fair view. In this case, the auditors would give an adverse opinion, stating that a true and fair view is not given. Here is an example of such a qualified opinion:

Adverse opinion

Basis for adverse opinion on financial statements

As more fully explained in note ... to the financial statements no provision has been made for losses expected to arise on certain long-term contracts currently in progress, as the directors consider that such losses should be offset against amounts recoverable on other long-term contracts. In our opinion, provision should be made for foreseeable losses on individual contracts as required by Statement of Standard Accounting Practice 9. If losses had been so recognised, the effect would have been to reduce the carrying amount of the contract work in progress by £X, deferred taxes payable by £Y and the profit for the year and retained earnings at 31 December 200X by £Z.

Adverse opinion on financial statements

In our opinion, because of the significance of the matter described in the basis for adverse opinion paragraph, the financial statements:

- do not give a true and fair view of the state of the company's affairs as at 31 December 20X1 and of its profit [loss] for the year then ended; and

- have not been properly prepared in accordance with United Kingdom Generally Accepted Accounting Practice.

In all other respects, in our opinion the financial statements have been prepared in accordance with the requirements of the Companies Act 2006.

Opinion on other matter prescribed by the Companies Act 2006

Notwithstanding our adverse opinion on the financial statements, in our opinion the information given in the Directors' Report for the financial year for which the financial statements are prepared is consistent with the financial statements.

Matters on which we are required to report by exception

[unchanged]

---

(3) There is a limitation of scope relating to a material item in financial statements, which means that the auditors are not able to express an opinion as to the truth and fairness of the financial statements in that

area. This matter is material to the financial statements, but not pervasive. Here is an example of such a qualified opinion:

Qualified opinion on financial statements arising from limitation in scope

Basis for qualified opinion on financial statements

With respect to inventory having a carrying amount of £X the audit evidence available to us was limited because we did not observe the counting of the physical inventory as at 31 December 20X1, since that date was prior to our appointment as auditor of the company. Owing to the nature of the company's records, we were unable to obtain sufficient appropriate audit evidence regarding the inventory quantities by using other audit procedures.

Qualified opinion on financial statements

In our opinion, except for the possible effects of the matters described in the basis for qualified opinion paragraph, the financial statements:

- give a true and fair view of the state of the company's affairs as at 31 December 200X and of its profit (loss) for the year then ended;

- have been properly prepared in accordance with United Kingdom Generally Accepted Accounting Practice; and

- have been prepared in accordance with the Companies Act 2006;

Opinion on other matter prescribed by the Companies Act 2006

In our opinion the information given in the Directors' Report for the financial year for which the financial statements are prepared is consistent with the financial statements.

Matters on which we are required to report by exception

In respect solely of the limitation on our work relating to inventory, described above:

- we have not obtained all the information and explanations that we considered necessary for the purpose of our audit; and

- we were unable to determine whether adequate accounting records had been kept.

We have nothing to report in respect of the following matters where the Companies Act 2006 requires us to report to you if, in our opinion:

- returns adequate for our audit have not been received from branches not visited by us; or

- the financial statements are not in agreement with the

---

accounting records and returns; or

- certain disclosures of directors' remuneration specified by law are not made.

(4) There is a substantial limitation on the work of the auditors which means that they are unable to give any opinion at all on the financial statements, so they give a disclaimer of opinion. Here is an example.

Basis of opinion (extract)

Basis for disclaimer of opinion on financial statements

The audit evidence available to us was limited because we were unable to observe the counting of physical inventory having a carrying amount of £X and send confirmation letters to trade receivables having a carrying amount of £Y due to limitations placed on the scope of our work by the directors of the company. As a result of this we have been unable to obtain sufficient appropriate audit evidence concerning both inventory and trade receivables.

Disclaimer of opinion on financial statements

Because of the significance of the matter described in the basis for disclaimer of opinion paragraph, we have not been able to obtain sufficient, appropriate audit evidence to provide a basis for an audit opinion. Accordingly we do not express an opinion on the financial statements:

Opinion on other matter prescribed by the Companies Act 2006

Notwithstanding our disclaimer of an opinion on the view given by the financial statements, in our opinion the information given in the Directors' Report for the financial year for which the financial statements are prepared is consistent with the financial statements.

Matters on which we are required to report by exception

In respect solely of the limitation of our work referred to above:

- we have not obtained all the information and explanations that we considered necessary for the purpose of our audit; and

- we were unable to determine whether adequate accounting records have been kept. We have nothing to report in respect of the following matters where the Companies Act 2006 requires us to report to you if, in our opinion:

- returns adequate for our audit have not been received from branches not visited by us; or

- the financial statements are not in agreement with the accounting records and returns; or

- certain disclosures of directors' remuneration specified by law are not made.

You should note that the auditor gives information about the reasons for modification. Problems are explained and, where possible, quantified.

Task 5

Imagine the following situations occurring on an audit.

(1) The sales director has included a material sale in the financial statements in order to meet his sales targets for the year, even though records clearly show that it was not transacted until the beginning of the next financial year and that the inventory was in the warehouse on the day of the inventory count. In the unamended financial statements, the inventory has been excluded from the closing inventory figure and the credit sale has been recognised. The sale value is £20,000 and the inventory value is £15,000.

(2) Two days before the audit was to take place the offices at the client burnt down and all the financial records were destroyed. The accountant has a set of financial statements for the year which he had prepared on his home computer.

Task

Draft appropriate audit report extracts for these two situations. You should only draft the sections of the report that would differ from the standard unqualified report.

Modified audit report with unmodified opinion

In accordance with ISA 706 *Emphasis of Matter and Other Matters Paragraphs in the Independent Auditor's Report*, the auditor's report may have a paragraph highlighting a **significant matter** in the financial statements, although such an emphasis of matter paragraph does not constitute a qualified opinion. An example of such a significant matter is a significant uncertainty.

Significant uncertainty

There may be a situation where the financial statements are affected by an uncertainty. An UNCERTAINTY is a matter whose outcome depends on future actions or events not under the direct control of the company but that may affect the financial statements.

If the potential impact of such an uncertainty is considered to be significant, the auditor should consider adding a paragraph to his auditor's report. Often this is the case if there is a significant level of concern about the going concern status of the company in connection with the uncertainty, for example, if the outcome of major litigation is pending.

The auditors need to consider whether any such uncertainty exists, and if it does, whether it is adequately accounted for and disclosed in the financial statements.

If a significant uncertainty exists, has been adequately accounted for and disclosed, the auditors will give an unqualified opinion, but will include an emphasis of matter paragraph in their auditor's report, bringing attention to the uncertainty. This is presented after the audit opinion. For example:

Emphasis of matter – going concern

In forming our opinion, which is not qualified, we have considered the adequacy of the disclosure made in note x to the financial statements concerning the company's ability to continue as a going concern. The company incurred a net loss of £X during the year ended 31 December 200X and, at that date, the company's current liabilities exceeded its total assets by £Y. These conditions, along with other matters explained in note x to the financial statements, indicate the existence of a material uncertainty which may cast significant doubt about the company's ability to continue as a going concern. The financial statements do not include the adjustments that would result if the company was unable to continue as a going concern.

Opinion on other matter prescribed by the Companies Act 2006

[rest of report unchanged]

If a significant uncertainty exists, but adequate accounting for and disclosure does not exist in the financial statements, then the financial statements do not give a true and fair view in this respect and the auditors would issue a qualified opinion.

Other reporting issues

We have touched on other areas that auditors will report about during the course of their audit – mainly reports made to management and directors about points arising during the audit.

Some professional standards set out the auditors' duties to report to certain parties in the event of unusual situations, such as the auditors suspecting or detecting a fraud. Remember, the auditors have a duty of confidentiality, so they must be very careful when making reports to persons outside the company.

Fraud

The auditors will have considered the possibility that the financial statements might be affected by misstatements as a result of fraud at the risk assessment stage of the audit. (See Chapter 5.)

If the auditors identify fraud or receive information that indicates a fraud exists during the course of the audit, then they should report that to the appropriate level of management as soon as possible:

    (1)   If it involves management or employees with significant roles in internal control

    (2)   Or if the fraud results in material misstatement in the financial statements

The auditors should inform the directors as soon as possible.

The auditors should only report frauds outside the entity if there is a **legal duty** to do so, otherwise they are at risk of breaching their duty of confidentiality.

It might be the case that a fraud resulted in money laundering taking place, in which situation the auditor is required to make an appropriate report to SOCA, and avoid tipping-off the client that he has done so, as outlined in Chapter 2. This may involve not making the reports outlined above.

Task 6

For each of the following situations which have arisen in two unrelated audit clients, select whether or not the auditor's opinion on the financial statements would be modified.

	Options
Gamma Ltd has included a warranty provision in the financial statements this year, having introduced a warranty to be offered to customers. The auditors have reviewed the warranty terms offered and believe the assumptions the provision is based on are fundamentally, materially wrong.	Modified Not modified
There is a significant uncertainty about Delta Ltd's ability to continue as a going concern. As the directors do not wish to make the situation any worse, they have not made any reference to going concern in the notes to the financial statements.	Modified Not modified

CHAPTER OVERVIEW

- Before they draw an audit opinion, auditors must carry out several additional reviews

- They must review the financial statements overall to ensure that they are consistent of themselves and with the auditors' understanding of the entity

- They must evaluate the materiality of uncorrected misstatements

- They must consider whether any events subsequent to the end of the reporting period have an effect on the financial statements and should be adjusted for or disclosed

- They must assess the directors' consideration of the going concern basis of the company and related disclosures in the financial statements

- There are several issues on which the auditors will require the directors to confirm representations made to them by the directors in writing

- The auditor's report must contain certain components according to professional standards

- The auditors will either give an unqualified opinion (when they believe the financial statements give a true or fair view) or a qualified one

- The auditors may modify the report if they disagree with something in the financial statements or if there has been a limitation on the scope of the audit due to an inability to obtain sufficient appropriate audit evidence

- The auditors may need to include an emphasis of matter paragraph in the audit report if there is a significant uncertainty affecting the financial statements

- Professional standards may impose other reporting requirements for auditors in unusual situations, such as when they uncover a fraud

Keyword

An **uncertainty** – a matter where outcome depends on future actions or events not under the direct control of the company but that may affect the financial statements

TEST YOUR LEARNING

Test 1 State whether the following statements are True or False.

	Options
Auditors must evaluate whether financial statements have been prepared in accordance with an applicable financial reporting framework.	True False
Auditors must use analytical procedures when determining if the financial statements appear reasonable as a whole.	True False

Test 2 Complete the following definition, by filling in the gaps using the items in the pick list below.

An entity is considered a ....
when it is likely to continue operating in the
....

Pick list

Good company

Going concern

Foreseeable future

Next year

Test 3 Auditors' responsibilities in respect of subsequent events differ depending on when such events occur.

Select when the auditors have the following responsibilities.

	Options
A responsibility to seek evidence of subsequent events and to ensure they are disclosed in financial statements.	Before auditor's report is signed After auditor's report is signed Both
A responsibility to seek evidence that the financial statements are fairly stated when management brings subsequent events to their attention.	Before auditor's report is signed After auditor's report is signed Both

Test 4 MEM is in the middle of legal action with a former employee for sexual discrimination. If the employee wins the action, the company could have to pay compensation that would have a material impact on the financial statements.

Task

Set out the implications of this legal action for the auditors.

Test 5 The auditors have reviewed the documentation from the solicitors about the legal action and have concluded that it appears probable that the compensation will have to be paid. They feel that the directors should provide for the compensation in the financial statements. The directors have refused.

Draft the opinion paragraph that should be included in the audit report in relation to this issue. You are not required to draft the section reporting to matters you would report by exception.

Test 6 For each of the following situations which have arisen in two unrelated audit clients, select whether or not the audit opinion on the financial statements would be modified.

	Options
The auditors have discovered aggregate misstatements of £25,000 on the audit of Spring Cleaners Ltd. Materiality has been set at £100,000. The directors refuse to amend the financial statements.	Modified Not modified
March Hare Ltd's largest customer has gone into liquidation. The directors do not want to write-off the debt owed by the customer which amounts to £25,000, which is material.	Modified Not modified

Test 7 During the audit of Sneaky Ltd, the audit senior discovered a file of invoices which did not appear to be included in the financial records, for which the company has been paid in cash. No VAT has been paid in relation to these sales.

Which one of the following is the most appropriate action for the audit senior to take?

Report the matter to:

- The board of directors
- HMRC
- The audit firm's money laundering reporting officer
- All of the above

ANSWERS TO CHAPTER TASKS

CHAPTER 1   The business environment

1   Major implications of registering a company are that the owners and the business are seen as separate entities, giving the owners certain benefits. These benefits include not being responsible for the company's debts.

   However, registering as a company means that the entity must also keep the requirements of the Companies Act.

2   Adequate accounting records are records sufficient to disclose with **reasonable accuracy**, the **financial position** of the company, **at all times**.

3   The directors need to keep records to enable a profit and loss account and balance sheet to be created at any time. This involves keeping records of:

   ■   Cash received and spent and details of what it relates to
   ■   Records of assets and liabilities

   If relevant:

   ■   Stock records for stock held at the year-end

   ■   Related stock count sheets

   ■   Records of goods bought/sold, showing the goods and seller or buyer (invoices)

4   False. Lilac Ltd is a private company, so it is required to keep records for at least three years after the date the record was created. Therefore, invoices from January 20X3 need to be kept until the beginning of February 20X6, and invoices from April 20X3 need to be kept until the beginning of May 20X6. If the company wants to dispose of this file as a whole, the file should not be disposed of for another five months (in May 20X6).

   True. Purple plc is a public limited company, so it is required to keep records for at least six years. Invoices from January 20X3 should be retained until the beginning of February 20X9. In other words, Purple plc should not dispose of this file for another three years and a month.

5   Third option. The companies required to have an audit are:

   Pear plc – because it is a public limited company

   Lime Ltd – because it has a turnover of greater than £6.5 million

   Lychee Ltd – because it is part of a group of companies

Lemon Ltd is exempt from audit because it is qualifies as a small company and Peach plc is exempt from audit because it qualifies as dormant.

CHAPTER 2   Introduction to audit

1   Audit evidence is conclusive not persuasive.   ✓

2   **True** is generally given to mean that **information** is factual and conforms with reality; it is not **false**. **Fair** is generally given to mean that information is free from **discrimination** and **bias** and is in compliance with expected **standards** and **rules**.

3   Auditors are required to state in a report whether financial statements give a true and fair view and have been properly prepared under UK GAAP and the Companies Act. They must report whether the directors' report is consistent with the financial statements. They should also report if adequate accounting records have not been kept or they have not received from client staff all the information and explanations they required for the purposes of their audit.

The auditors are given the right to expect all the information and explanations from client staff auditors feels are necessary for the purposes of their audit. They are also entitled to access all the books and records of the company. They have the right to be told about company meetings, to attend such meetings and speak on matters that affected them as auditors.

4

▪ Company	Automatic
▪ Bank	Must be proved
▪ Individual shareholder	Must be proved
▪ Creditor	Must be proved

The auditors do owe a duty of care to the client, that is the shareholders as a body (the company) automatically under UK law. It is always possible that they may also owe a duty of care to other parties, such as the bank, individual shareholders and creditors, if those parties have established a special relationship with the auditors.

5   Compare your answer to the list given in the next section of the chapter.

6   Compare your answer to the answers given in the next section of the chapter.

7   It is appropriate to discuss client affairs in the audit firm premises and in private at the client's premises (for example, a private meeting room).

There are many places where it is inappropriate to discuss client affairs, particularly public places, regardless of their proximity to the client, so client affairs should never be discussed in any restaurant. In addition, it is inappropriate to discuss client affairs in certain places at the client, such as if the directors have told the auditors information that other staff members do not know, the auditors should not discuss client affairs in public in the client's accounts department. Clearly, they are entitled to ask client staff questions relevant to carrying out the audit task at hand, but they must be sensitive to confidential information.

8   Albert should ideally not leave audit files in the car, he should go home first and put them away there. However, if it is necessary to leave the car for a brief period, the files should be locked up in a case and secured in the boot of the car.

Beth has behaved appropriately in this situation. It was not possible for her to lock the door of the office, but she has taken precautions against the files being read by other people.

Clare and Daniel should not discuss client affairs in the pub. They should wait until they are back at the client's premises.

The security arrangements over the older files of Edwards Auditors Co are appropriate. They should take care that the code to get into the storage room is kept confidential.

CHAPTER 3   The company environment (controls)

1

	Options
Management prefer favourable to honest reporting within the business.	Weak
Management take the lead in enforcing control values.	Strong

2   A larger company may have a written code of conduct about internal controls, whereas it is unlikely that a smaller company will. In a small company, directors may work closely with operational staff and their attitude to controls will be particularly influential.

3   **Business risks at MEM**

(1)   Reporting properly

The fact that the qualified accountant is not on the board may impair the effectiveness of the board to report properly.

The fact that the company deals in more than one currency increases the risk of errors in the financial statements.

(2) Operating properly

The business is at risk of not operating properly due to out-of-date machinery.

In addition, the company is facing increased competition from a company which is likely to have more up-to-date equipment and may have a useful knowledge of MEM's operating practices.

(3) Keeping the law

The company has a number of employees and must ensure that it keeps the many legal requirements in relation to its employees.

The company operates from an old building using old machines. It must ensure that it operates within the boundaries of health and safety law as well.

4 There is very little segregation of duties at HEC and, although the key sales and purchase functions are carried out by the directors, the system would benefit from some segregation being introduced. For example, payments for purchases should be carried out or authorised by someone other than Rosemary.

5 The answer follows the task in the chapter text below it.

6 Examples of controls are given in the next section of the chapter.

7 The answer follows the task in the chapter text below it.

8 Credit checks on new customers are to ensure that the customer is a good credit risk and able to pay debts. Sales invoices should be sequentially numbered to ensure that fictitious sales invoices are not raised (and used to then misappropriate genuine payments for other invoices). Receivables' statements should be prepared regularly to check that the sales ledger has been kept correctly (customers are likely to draw attention to debts that are not genuine) and to encourage customers to pay promptly. There should be restrictions on who is allowed to receive cash for the business to minimise the risk of cash being stolen or lost.

9 ▪ Sales orders should be recorded on pre-numbered documents

▪ Despatch notes should be checked to sales orders prior to despatch

▪ The sales ledger should be written-up more frequently to aid credit control

▪ Sales ledger should be reviewed frequently to check for irrecoverable receivables

▪ Someone other than Peter should record and bank receipts

10 The answer follows the task in the chapter text below it.

11 Examples of controls are given in the next section of the chapter.

12 The answer follows the task in the chapter text below it.

13 The necessity for orders should be evidenced so that goods are only purchased for genuine business reasons. Supplier invoices should be referenced so that they can be recorded in sequence and so that they can be recovered easily in the event of disputes. Supplier statements should be compared to the purchase ledger to discover errors in recording in the purchase ledger and/or to discover whether the company is being charged for genuine liabilities. Blank cheques should never be signed as this makes it easier for cash to be stolen from the company/spent on goods which are not for business use.

14 The answer follows the task in the chapter text below it.

15 Examples of controls are given in the next section of the chapter.

16 The answer follows the task in the chapter text below it.

17 Changes in personnel should be recorded so that the right employees are paid for work done. A payroll should be prepared to ensure that employees are paid the correct amounts and the correct deductions are made, and posting to the general ledger can be checked. A wage cheque for cash payments should be authorised so that cash is not stolen. Costs of pay should be compared to budgets because any discrepancies observed might reveal errors in calculation or in payments made to staff or leavers inappropriately.

18 The answer follows the task in the chapter text below it.

19 Examples of controls are given in the next section of the chapter.

20 The answer follows the task in the chapter text below it.

21 Capital expenditure is authorised to prevent people purchasing assets to benefit themselves rather than the business, and to make sure the correct asset is purchased at an appropriate price at the correct time in terms of the company's cash flow and business needs. Assets should be inspected regularly to check that they still exist and are in use to the business (or their value will be affected) and that they are in good condition to be used. Asset scrappage should be authorised so that the item can be scrapped at an appropriate time (ie when it has been replaced) and also to ensure that it is scrapped appropriately, and for the correct money if sold.

22 The answer follows the task in the chapter text below it.

23 Examples of controls are given in the next section of the chapter.

24 Access to stores should be restricted to reduce the threat of inventory being stolen. Inventory should be counted regularly to ensure that actual inventory conforms to what the company has recorded as inventory levels. The condition of inventory should be checked to ensure that it still has value to the business (in use or for sale) and to ensure that valuation is correct.

Reorder limits should be set so that the company does not run out of items of inventory causing business interruption.

CHAPTER 4   Auditing systems

1   Internal control questionnaire

Metal Extrusions Midlands Limited

Purchases system

Question	Y/N	Comment
Is there a central policy for choosing suppliers?		
Are purchase requisitions produced for all purchase orders and authorised by department heads?		
Are all orders raised as a result of an authorised purchase requisition?		
Are all orders completed on pre-numbered order forms?		
Are blank order forms kept securely?		
Are outstanding orders reviewed regularly and chased up?		
Are supplier terms monitored?		
Are goods received examined for quantity and quality?		
Are goods received recorded on pre-numbered goods received notes?		
Are goods received notes compared with purchase orders?		
Are supplier invoices checked to orders and goods received notes?		
Are supplier invoices referenced by the company?		
Are supplier invoices checked for price, quantity and correct calculations?		
Are goods returns recorded on pre-numbered goods returned notes?		

Question	Y/N	Comment
Does the company have procedures for obtaining credit notes from suppliers?		
Are purchases and purchase returns recorded promptly in daybooks and ledgers?		
Is the purchase ledger maintained regularly?		
Are payments authorised only if goods have been received?		
Is the purchase ledger control account reconciled to the list of balances?		
Are goods received but not yet invoiced accrued separately at the year-end?		
Are cheques requisitioned with appropriate supporting information?		
Are cheque payments authorised by someone other than a cheque signatory?		
Are there monetary limits on the amounts individual staff members can authorise/sign?		
Are there suitable controls to prevent signing of blank cheques?		
Are signed cheques dispatched promptly?		
Does the company collect paid cheques from the bank?		
Are payments recorded promptly in the cashbook and ledger?		
Are cash payments limited and authorised?		

2   The auditor can confirm the system operates as it has been set out by watching a transaction pass through that system.

3   Any five from the following answers:

Task 1	Task 2
Controls operating in the system	*Potential tests of that control*
Sales staff check that outstanding orders are not in excess of the credit amount before taking orders	If possible in the system, review order volumes for each client on a month-by-month basis to see if any breaches of limits are indicated. Confirm whether any references to the check on the sales order have been made
Orders are recorded on pre-numbered sales orders	Review a sample of orders to ensure that they are pre-numbered

Task 1	Task 2
Controls operating in the system	*Potential tests of that control*
Only Ted is allowed to authorise sales orders over £20,000	Select a sample of sales invoices in excess of £20,000 and trace to the sales orders to check who authorised them
Only Ted is allowed to authorise new customers after a credit check has been carried out	Check that a credit check was carried out and that Ted authorised the customer by reference to a sample of new customer files
Ian Mellor checks goods to be despatched for quantity and quality	Observe Ian Mellor carrying out such checks. Review a sample of goods despatch notes to see if they are marked as having been checked
Invoices created from goods despatch notes and matching sales order	Review a selection of sales invoices in the accounts department to ensure that they are matched with GRNs and orders
Prices are automatically inserted on the invoice	Observe Tessa processing invoices
The production of invoices automatically triggers updating of the sales daybook and ledger	Observe Tessa processing invoices. Review the sales daybook and ledger afterwards to ensure updated
Post is opened by two people	Observe the post opening routine
Processing the cashbook automatically updates the sales ledger for receipts	Review the sales ledger after cash book update to ensure this is the case
The financial controller reconciles the sales ledger control account on a monthly basis	Look at evidence of this reconciliation having taken place
Tessa Goodyear reviews an aged debt report for potentially irrecoverable receivables weekly	Review her weekly reports if possible (if she retains them). Review any correspondence with customers or the debt collection agency. Observe Tessa carrying out her credit control routines on Monday mornings

4   D – the key control is that the purchase has been authorised, therefore the auditors need to seek evidence that that authorisation took place.

5

	Options
Extraction of all receivables balances older than 120 days to perform irrecoverable receivable work.	Audit software
Input of purchase invoices with false customer numbers to ensure that the system rejects the invoices.	Test data
Comparison of suppliers on ledger with previous years to discover any new or missing suppliers.	Audit software

6   **Strengths/deficiencies/both**

(1)   Only Ted Bishop is allowed to authorise new customers and orders over £20,000.

Both. It is good that there is a control over larger purchases, but the fact that it is restricted to one person, means that if Ted Bishop is ill or on holiday customers may be kept waiting and ultimately lost, which is a weakness in the system.

(2)   Orders are recorded on pre-numbered sales orders.

Strength. Orders should not get lost and therefore be unfulfilled.

(3)   Goods are sometimes ready for despatch early.

Deficiency. This suggests weaknesses in the system to determine when goods can be produced by and may mean that goods have to be stored on MEM's premises at MEM's risk until they can be despatched to the customer. It also adds to the delay between MEM spending money on raw materials and recouping money on sales. The initial prediction of production time should be more accurate.

(4)   It is necessary for Tessa to manually override the price system on the computer if a special price has been negotiated.

Deficiency. This is a weakness as it means that the good controls over price input can be overridden for other reasons too. It might be better if the sales department set up any special prices agreed within the system and gave notice to Tessa of the appropriate code. However, controls would need to be exercised over this addition to standing data on the computer.

7   Report on internal control deficiencies (extracts)

Weakness: delivery notes

At present, delivery notes do not appear to be retained and matched with invoices.

Implication

Goods delivered and goods invoiced may not match up, meaning that the company may be paying for goods which it has not received.

Recommendation

Delivery notes should be retained and sent to Rosemary, who should check that invoices and goods delivered agree before they are ready for payment. She should keep two files – one, 'invoices received' and another 'invoices ready for payment' and invoices should not be paid until they have been matched with a delivery note.

Weakness: lack of segregation of duties

At present, Rosemary is in charge of choosing suppliers, making orders, authorising invoices for payment, writing and signing cheques and recording payments.

Implication

Rosemary could make errors in ordering or recording which might not be picked up by another member of staff. Consequently, there is additional scope for a fraud being carried out on the company if no other staff members are involved in the system.

Recommendation

Some other person should be involved in the system. As a minimum, Peter should authorise purchase ledger payments. There should be a monetary limit over which cheques need to be countersigned by Peter. It might be better to get a member of staff other than Rosemary to prepare payments on the purchase ledger as well.

Weakness: invoicing

At present, invoices are sent to various people and places in the company.

Implication

Invoices may be lost or delayed being transferred to Rosemary, especially as the business operates from a number of sites. This might result in suppliers being paid late or not at all, it might also result in the company not benefiting from early payment discounts.

Recommendation

Suppliers should be requested to bill Rosemary at the High Street branch for all purchases, regardless of where goods are delivered or collected from.

CHAPTER 5   Assessing risks

1

If inherent and control risk have been determined to be high, auditors will have to carry out a high level of testing to render overall audit risk acceptable.	True – as detection risk will be low, which means a high level of testing must be carried out.
If inherent and control risk have been determined to be high, auditors will judge that detection risk must be low.	True – this is really saying the same thing as the first option.

2

	Options
Performance materiality should be set at less than materiality for the financial statements as a whole.	True
Materiality is a measure of the importance of items to a reader of financial statements.	True
Items may be material due to their size, nature or effect on the financial statements.	True

3

There is an error in receivables, value £7,500.	Material
A loan to a director has been disclosed in the financial statement at £2,000. Actually the correct sum is £2,010.	Material
The company is required to keep a current asset ratio of 2:1. An error of £100 has been found in receivables, which will cause the ratio to drop below this level.	Material

4

	Options
The entity is to be sold and the purchase consideration will be determined as a multiple of reported profit.	Increase
The company has a history of being slow to follow new accounting standards and guidance.	Increase

5 Incentives/pressures

Financial stability or profitability is threatened by economic, industry or entity operating conditions, such as or indicated by:

- High degree of competition
- Vulnerability to rapid changes
- Decline in customer demand/business failures in industry
- Operating losses/recurring negative cash flows
- Rapid growth or unusual profitability compared to others in the industry
- New accounting or statutory requirements

Excessive pressure to meet the requirements of third parties due to:

- Profitability expectations (shareholders/the stock market generally)
- Need to obtain additional funding
- Marginal ability to meet listing requirements
- Affect of poor financial results on pending transactions

Connection of company performance with management's own situation:

- Significant financial interests in the entity
- Significant portions of compensation contingent on performance
- Personal guarantees for entity debts

Incentives or pressures to misappropriate assets:

- Personal financial obligations
- Poor relationships between management and staff

Excessive pressure on staff to meet targets

Opportunities

Nature of the entity makes it more straightforward to conduct fraud:

- Significant related party transactions
- Strong presence in an industry allowing domination
- Necessity for significant estimates in financial reporting
- Unusual or complex transactions
- Operations across several international boundaries
- Use of business intermediaries with no clear justification
- Significant bank accounts in tax havens with no justification

Ineffective monitoring of management:

- Domination of management by a single person
- Ineffective oversight by management
- Complex corporate structure
- Deficient internal control
- Characteristics of assets lend themselves to misappropriation

Attitudes/rationalisations

- Failure to communicate company ethical policy
- Low morale
- No distinction made by owner-manager between business/personal transactions

6

The entity is committed to employing skilled personnel in the accounts department.	Reduce
The company prepares detailed budgets and analyses variances from budgets closely.	Reduce
The entity's management has not remedied deficiencies in internal control noted by the auditors in the past.	Increase

CHAPTER 6   Audit planning

1

	Options
Trade receivables has increased by 25% and revenue has increased by 7%	Overstated
Trade payables has decreased by 5% and purchases has increased by 4%	Understated

2

	Options
Inspecting purchase orders for evidence that the additions and calculations have been checked.	Test of control
Recalculating a depreciation charge.	Substantive procedure
Comparing month on month sales to the previous year.	Substantive procedure

3

	Options
Terms of the agreement.	Rights and obligations
Total amount on the agreement.	Valuation

4

	Options
Auditors intend to increase reliance on the company's system of internal control for the purposes of the audit.	Increase
Auditors believe that there is likely to be a higher deviation rate in controls due to a new member of staff.	Increase
Increased activity in the factory and new customers, resulting in 25% more sales invoices being issued during the year.	No effect

5

	Options
Obtain evidence that sales have not been understated.	Sales order
Obtain evidence that sales have not been overstated.	Sales ledger

CHAPTER 7   Audit of inventory

1   True. It is an inherent risk of inventory.

2   The problem will be that there is a large number of different inventory lines and they are kept in various different locations, including a third party location.

3   The auditors will have to consider whether:

- The basis used to allocate original cost is reasonable

- The standard cost calculation is reasonable

- It is reasonable to apply the same standard cost to each item of inventory

4   I will need to consider:

- Whether the count instructions are adequate and indicate that controls over the count will be good

- What the key factors are (location, high value items)

- What procedures I intend to carry out at the count

5   NRV and cost are likely to be the same as the company has not added any value to the raw materials in terms of production. However, if raw materials have been kept for a long time they may have reduced in value.

6   Factors include:

- An increase in costs or a fall in selling price
- Physical deterioration in inventories
- Obsolescence of products
- Decision as part of a marketing strategy to sell goods at a loss
- Errors in production or purchasing

7   A   £20,000 (part X at cost and part Y at NRV)

CHAPTER 8   Audit of other assets (and related items)

1   The answer to this question is given in the following text in the chapter.

2   **High Street shop**

- Look at the title deeds to confirm that HEC owns the shop

- Check the value in the financial statements agrees to the valuation by the surveyor and consider whether the valuation is reasonable

- Check the calculation of depreciation has been done correctly subsequent to the valuation by recalculating it

- Visit the shop to confirm that it exists

Delivery van

- Look at the registration documents to ensure the company owns the van

- Agree cost to the purchase invoice or to last year's file if the company owned the van last year

- Check the calculation of depreciation

- Inspect the van to ensure it exists

Shop fittings

- Check the purchase invoices to ensure that the company owns the fittings and the cost is correct. Alternatively, if the assets were owned last year, this can be verified to last year's file

- Inspect the fittings to ensure they exist

3

Client:	HEC		Prepared by:	Student
Accounting date:	31 December 20X8		Date:	8 April 20X9
			Reviewed by:	
			Date:	

Trade receivables

Receivable	Balance per sales ledger	Receipts after date (Jan)	Receipts after date (Feb)	Reconciled?
Grand Hotel	10,593	4,569	**6,024**	**Yes**
Happy Eatin'	9,967	4,792	5,175	Yes
Secret Garden	**6,898**	–	3,892	**No**
Quinn's	2,831	–	–	No
Victorine's	**1,936**	1,936	938*	Yes

* Balance reconciled in January.

Further work required

Victorine's – check that £938 relates to January invoices.

Secret Garden – check whether £3,892 received relates to an invoice or group of invoices and ensure that oldest invoices have been paid. Ensure outstanding balance also relates to an invoice or group of invoices.

Quinns – check how old the balance is and what Quinn's past pattern of payment has been. If it appears the debt may be doubtful, discuss with Peter Tyme to see if action has been taken and whether the debt has been provided against.

If debt appears doubtful and no adjustment has been made, the following journal should be made:

Dr **Irrecoverable receivable Expense**	£2,831	
Cr **Receivables**		£2,831

4   Tests over completeness of sales

The auditor should perform analytical procedures on sales levels month-by-month and compare them to previous years to see if sales appear reasonable.

In addition, due to the increased risk of cash sales not being recorded, a sample of sales from original documents to the general ledger should be traced through.

At HEC, the original documents are the book in which sales are recorded and the till rolls. A sample of sales should be traced from these to the sales ledger and the general ledger.

5   **Bank balance at HEC**

- Obtain a bank letter from HEC's bank confirming the balance

- Obtain a copy of the bank reconciliation and check its mathematical accuracy

- Trace outstanding payments to after-date bank statements and ensure that they clear in reasonable time

- Trace receipts not yet cleared to ensure that they clear in reasonable time

- Review the bank statements and cashbook for items not appearing in the other and unusual items and discuss them with management, if required

Cash balances at HEC

The cash floats at the shops are likely to be reasonably large, although they may not be material.

Arrange to check the cash in each of the tills at the same time. It will probably be preferable to HEC that this is done after hours.

The cash check does not need to be done on the year-end date as it is a test of the controls over the cash balance rather than the actual value of the balance.

6   **B** – The Princes and Gaston balances should be included.

The Staceys balance of £24,000 appears on the ledger at 31 December and subsequently in error, as the credit note issued on 30 December should have cancelled this balance from the ledger. Further checks should be carried out to ensure how this credit note was accounted for and whether this problem has been repeated elsewhere.

The Ariel balance existed at the year-end, but clearly the customer was questioning the company's right to that money as there was a dispute which has eventually resulted in a credit note being issued. This means that the company did not have the right to the receivable at the year-end, and it should not be included in receivables.

CHAPTER 9   Audit of liabilities (and related items)

1   Supplier statements represent good evidence for the auditors as they are generated by a third party.

2

Client:	MEM		Prepared by:	Student
Accounting date:	31 December 20X8		Date:	9 April 20X9
			Reviewed by:	
			Date:	

Trade payables

Supplier	Balance per purchase ledger £	Balance per supplier statement £	Balance agreed	Comments
Applewoods	10,473	10,473	Yes	
Brilliant Butchers Limited	3,793	3,793	Yes	
Deepa's Delicacies Limited	587	587	Yes	
Hot Chocolate Limited	34			No supplier statement available
Keil Farm Organics	9,572	12,990	No	Invoice for £3,418
Ordinary Organics Limited	392	392	Yes	
Peterwoods Farm Limited	493			No supplier statement available
Steepdale Farm	3,947	3,947	Yes	
Taylors' Farm Produce Limited	8,351	8,351	Yes	
Very Nice Food Limited	277			No supplier statement available

Further work required

Alternative procedures should be carried out on the three balances for which no supplier statement is available. None of the items is high value. Sufficient evidence may be given by verifying these amounts to invoices and verifying that invoices prior to these had been paid at 31 December and those subsequent were genuinely liabilities arising after the year-end. Alternatively, it might be considered necessary to circularise these suppliers, particularly as controls over purchases are not strong.

In respect of Keil Farm, we must scrutinise the invoice which Keil believe is due at the year-end to ascertain whether it has been accounted for in the correct period. We must review both the invoice and the goods received note if possible. If it appears that the invoice should have been included in 20X8, we should ask the directors to adjust the financial statements for this invoice.

3   The following work should be carried out on the loan:

■ Obtain a schedule showing what is due in more than one year and what is due in less than one year.

■ Test the calculations to ensure that this analysis is correct, that interest has been treated correctly and that the total balance payable agrees to the bank letter.

■ Ensure that appropriate disclosure has been made in the financial statements.

4   D £45,000. The company has made a payment before the year-end which does not reach the supplier until after the year-end (but the timing of its banking does tally with a pre-year-end payment. In addition, the supplier has acknowledged it has no right to the debt in respect of the December invoice which it later issues a credit note against.

CHAPTER 10 Audit completion and reporting

1 Analytical procedures will be very helpful in determining whether the financial statements as a whole give a coherent picture. The auditor can calculate ratios and compare items with significant relationships (such as sales and receivables) to ascertain whether the picture appears reasonable. The financial statements can also be compared with previous years.

2 Examples of use of post year end information:

- Use of cash receipts to confirm valuation of debts
- Use of after-date cheque presentation to confirm bank reconciliation
- Use of after-date payments to confirm existence of liabilities

3 Factors indicating that the company might not be a going concern:

Financial

- Net liabilities or net current liability position
- Necessary borrowing facilities have not been arranged
- Major restructuring of debt
- Indications of withdrawal of financial support by customers/lenders
- Negative operating cash flows
- Adverse key financial ratios
- Substantial operating losses
- Arrears/discontinuance of dividends
- Inability to pay lenders on due dates/reduction in normal credit terms
- Inability to comply with terms of loan agreements

Operational

- Loss of key management/staff without replacement
- Loss of a major market, franchise, license or supplier
- Labour difficulties, shortage of key supplies
- Fundamental changes in technology or market
- Excessive dependence on a few product lines when market is depressed
- Technical developments rendering a key product obsolete

Other

- Non-compliance with legal requirements
- Pending legal proceedings which could result in ruin
- Changes in legislation expected to adversely affect the entity

4 This activity requires that you do something. There is no answer that can be given here.

5 **Issue 1**

> ### Qualified opinion arising from disagreement about accounting treatment
>
> ### Basis for qualified opinion on financial statements
>
> Included in turnover is a sale of £20,000 made after the year-end. In our opinion this sale should be included in sales in the next accounting period and the inventory should be accounted for in the balance sheet, which would have reduced sales and trade receivables by £20,000 and increased inventory in the balance sheet and the profit and loss account by £15,000.
>
> ### Qualified opinion on financial statements
>
> In our opinion, except for the effects of to the matter described in the basis for qualified opinion paragraph, in our opinion the financial statements:
>
> - Give a true and fair view of the state of the company's affairs as at 31 December 200X and of its profit for the year then ended.
>
> - Have been properly prepared in accordance with United Kingdom Generally Accepted Accounting Practice, and
>
> - Have been prepared in accordance with the Companies Act 2006.

Issue 2

> ### Basis for disclaimer of opinion on financial statements
>
> The audit evidence available to us was limited because the accounting records were destroyed by fire prior to the commencement of the audit.
>
> ### Disclaimer of opinion on financial statements
>
> Because of the significance of the matter described in the basis for disclaimer of opinion paragraph, we have not been able to obtain sufficient, appropriate audit evidence to provide a basis for an audit opinion. Accordingly we do not express an opinion on the financial statements:
>
> ### Opinion on other matter prescribed by the Companies Act 2006
>
> Notwithstanding our disclaimer of an opinion on the view given by the financial statements, in our opinion the information given in the Directors' Report for the financial year for which the financial statements are prepared is consistent with the financial statements.
>
> ### Matters on which we are required to report by exception
>
> In respect of the limitation of our work referred to above:
>
> - we have not obtained all the information and explanations that we considered necessary for the purpose of our audit; and
>
> - we were unable to determine whether adequate accounting records have been kept.

- we were unable to determine whether the financial statements are in agreement with the accounting records and returns

We have nothing to report in respect of the following matters where the Companies Act 2006 requires us to report to you if, in our opinion:

- returns adequate for our audit have not been received from branches not visited by us; or

- the financial statements are not in agreement with the accounting records and returns; or

- certain disclosures of directors' remuneration specified by law are not made.

6

	Options
Gamma Ltd has included a warranty provision in the financial statements this year, having introduced a warranty to be offered to customers. The auditors have reviewed the warranty terms offered and believe the assumptions the provision is based on are fundamentally, materially wrong.	Modified – this is a material disagreement about an accounting policy.
There is a significant uncertainty about Delta Ltd's ability to continue as a going concern. As the directors do not wish to make the situation any worse, they have not made any reference to going concern in the notes to the financial statements.	Modified for non disclosure of the significant uncertainty about going concern.

Answers to chapter tasks

TEST YOUR LEARNING – ANSWERS

CHAPTER 1   The business environment

1   A **company** is an entity registered as such under the Companies Act 2006.

2   The last statement is incorrect. A company does not have to be managed by its owners. However, registering a company does means that it is seen as a separate entity from its owners, and that it must satisfy certain requirements of the Companies Act, such as keeping accounting records and having its financial statements audited.

3   True

   False – only those companies that deal in goods need fulfil this requirement (other companies have no stock (inventory) to record).

   False – public limited companies should keep accounting records for six years. Private limited companies should keep accounting records for three years.

4   Puma Limited – not exempt

   Jaguar plc – exempt – dormant

   Cheetah Limited – not exempt (as it is part of a group)

   Lion plc – not exempt (as it is a plc)

5   Leopard Limited must keep adequate financial records. As it is a manufacturing company, this will include records of stock as well as of assets and liabilities, cash received and spent and details of these cash movements.

   Leopard Limited is also required to have an audit of its financial statements. This is because Leopard Limited does not qualify as a small company, as its balance sheet total is greater than £3.26 million.

CHAPTER 2 Introduction to audit

1   An **audit** is an exercise carried out by **auditors** to ascertain whether the **financial statements** prepared by the **directors** are (in the UK) in accordance with the UK GAAP and the **Companies Act 2006** and give what is known as a **true and fair view**.

2   True
    True
    True

3   The client and any other parties with whom they have implied a special relationship.

4   A duty of care existed, it was breached, causing loss.

5   Quality control standards, ethical standards, engagement standards (ISAs UK&I), practice notes, bulletins

6   **Confidentiality** is the duty to keep **client** affairs **private**.

7   The auditors must keep their work secure, so that they can keep client affairs private.

8   Working papers are the record of audit work done.

CHAPTER 3   The company environment (controls)

1   **Internal control** is the process **designed**, implemented and **maintained** by **those charged with governance**, **management** and other personnel to provide **reasonable assurance** about the achievement of the entity's **objectives** with regard to the reliability of **financial reporting**, effectiveness and efficiency of **operations** and compliance with applicable laws and regulations

2   Control objective
Risk
Control procedure

3   The directors can ensure a good control environment by implementing controls themselves and never bypassing them. True

The directors should not assign authority for control areas to members of staff. False

A good control environment always leads to a good system of control overall. False – not necessarily, although a good control environment would usually suggest that the control system is strong.

4   A large company is more likely to have a good control environment than a small company. Control environment depends on the attitudes, awareness and actions of directors. Although some small companies may have difficulties in activating controls such as segregation of duties due to staff restrictions, the attitudes of management will not necessarily be poorer just because the company is small.

In practice, control activities will be similar in all sizes of company over core activities, although all companies differ and have some varying objectives, so controls will alter from company to company to some extent. Large and small companies are likely to be different in terms of the formality of their control environment, or the formality and extent of their information systems.

5   D. Who monitors controls will vary from company to company. Larger companies may have internal audit functions, one of whose key purposes will be to monitor controls. In small companies, control monitoring is less likely to be formal and is likely to be carried out by the staff in charge of each function or department.

6   Key objectives in a sales system (any of):

(1)   Goods and services only supplied to good credit risks
(2)   Customers encouraged to pay promptly
(3)   Orders recorded accurately
(4)   Orders fulfilled correctly
(5)   All despatches of goods recorded
(6)   Goods and services sold invoiced

(7)   Invoices raised relate to goods/services sold

(8)   Credit notes only given for valid reasons

(9)   Invoiced sales and credit notes recorded in the accounting records

(10) Entries in sales ledger made to the correct accounts

(11) Entries in sales ledger made in the correct period

(12) Potentially doubtful debts identified

7   Controls (numbers as in answer 6 – some of these objectives can be met by a single control):

(1)   Credit checks carried out for new customers, orders only accepted from customers with no existing payment difficulties

(2)   Credit terms set out on invoice, receivables' statements prepared and sent regularly

(3)   Orders recorded on documents with sequential numbering

(4)   Matching of orders with productions orders/despatch notes prior to despatch, goods checked for quantity/quality before despatch

(5)   Despatches recorded on pre-numbered goods despatch notes

(6)   Invoices matched to despatch notes, regular review of unmatched despatch notes

(7)   Invoices matched to despatch notes and delivery documentation signed by customer

(8)   Credit notes authorised by senior personnel, review of returned goods

(9)   Matching of invoices to despatch notes and delivery documentation

(10) Regular preparation of receivables' statements, review of ledger for unpaid debts

(11) Review of unmatched despatch notes and inventory records

(12) Regular review of ledger for unpaid debts

8   Purchases system at HEC

Controls present:

- Rosemary keeps a record of all purchases in the purchases order book
- Paid invoices are marked with a P

Potential additional controls:

- Orders noted on pre-numbered order documents

- Delivery or goods received notes retained/matched with invoices

- Segregation of duties between ordering and payment introduced

- All suppliers asked to bill Rosemary directly

- Cheques countersigned, or authorised by someone other than Rosemary

9   Control objectives over wages:

(1)   Employees only paid for work done
(2)   Gross pay calculated correctly and authorised
(3)   Gross pay, net pay and deductions correctly recorded on payroll
(4)   Wages and salaries paid recorded properly in bank records
(5)   Wages and salaries recorded correctly in the general ledger
(6)   Deductions calculated correctly and authorised
(7)   The correct amounts paid to the taxation authorities

10

Internal control procedure	Control objective
The payroll should be reconciled to other records, such as the cash payment for net pay per the bank.	Gross pay, net pay and deductions should be correctly recorded on payroll
The payroll should be authorised by someone other than the personnel director	Gross pay should be calculated correctly and authorised

11

Internal control procedure	Risk mitigated
Non current assets are inspected regularly	Assets are not maintained properly for use in the business
Capital expenditure is approved by the purchasing director on behalf of the board	Assets are bought from inappropriate suppliers at inflated cost

12

Internal control procedure	Risk mitigated
Inventory store is kept locked	Inventory is stolen
Goods inwards are checked for quality	Damaged inventory is valued in the financial statements

CHAPTER 4   Auditing systems

1   –   Auditors ascertain the client's system by a combination of **observation** and **enquiry**.

        –   Auditors confirm that the system operates as intended by conducting a **walkthrough test**.

        –   If auditors believe that the control system is strong, they will take a **combined** approach to the audit.

        –   If auditors believe the control system to be weak, they will take a more **substantive** approach to the audit.

2

	Options
A series of questions designed to identify controls in a system. A no answer indicates a weakness in controls	ICQ
A graphic rendition of the system, using conventional symbols to represent controls and documents	Flowchart

3

	Options
The systems notes should be easy to follow at a glance and easy to review	Flowchart
The systems notes should be comprehensive and detailed, and, if computerised, easy to update	Narrative notes
The systems notes should follow the firm's standard and should be easy for staff to use	Questionnaire

4

	Options
A yes answer to an internal control questionnaire indicates that a control exists	True
A yes answer to an internal control questionnaire indicates that the auditors can rely on a control in the system for the purposes of their audit	False. The control system must still be evaluated before the auditor makes that judgement.

5

	Options
When an auditor evaluates an internal control system he is concerned with the design of internal controls.	True
When an auditor evaluates an internal control system he is concerned with the operation of internal controls.	True

6   Computer-assisted audit techniques are methods of obtaining **evidence** by using **computers**

Audit software is **software** that can check **data** on computer systems by **interrogating** or by comparing versions of **programmes**.

Test data is a way of checking computer **programming** by inputting real or false information and observing how the programme deals with it.

7

	Options
Observe post opening	Test of control
Safeguard blank purchase order forms	Control activity
Review numerical sequence of goods received notes	Test of control

8   Weaknesses: goods received

Goods are not necessarily received into MEM by staff members who know anything about the goods. They do not appear to be examined for quantity or quality. They are not recorded on pre-numbered goods received notes and no check is made against the order.

Implications

MEM may habitually accept poor quality goods or goods which do not match up to the order, causing delays in production (resulting in the problems noted above) and potentially, unjustified cost to MEM.

Recommendations

(1)   Purchase orders should be three-part documents and one copy should be sent to the warehouse. This copy can be discarded as soon as goods have been received and checked.

(2)   Regardless of who accepts the goods, they should be checked for quantity against the purchase order and where possible for quality. If any doubt arises, the person should not accept the goods but send for the appropriate personnel to check for quality.

(3) Goods received should be noted on two-part goods received notes which should be sent to the purchases office for matching with purchase orders. When an order has been matched it should be filed (as discussed above) and the goods received note should be marked as agreed to order and sent to the accounts department for matching with an invoice (see below).

Weakness: purchase invoices

Purchase invoices are not currently checked to goods received notes. Iain Davies does not check any of the details of the invoices.

Implications

Suppliers could charge in error and MEM would not pick this up. They might pay invoices that have been wrongly calculated or for goods that they have not in fact received. The check that is carried out against supplier statements will not pick up supplier errors.

Recommendations

Invoices should be matched with goods received notes before they are processed. Iain should also check (and show that he has checked by initialling or stamping the invoices) the details on supplier invoices.

9   Task 1

Weakness: Failure to compare actual payroll costs to budget

No-one compares the cost of the payroll (wages, salaries, costs of employers' NI, any company pension contributions) to the budgeted cost at the start of the year.

Implication

Errors may arise in the payroll (which could be highlighted by such comparison) and not be corrected which might result in overpayment of wages or of tax.

Recommendation

The payroll costs should be compared to budget on a monthly basis and variances investigated. The review should probably be carried out by Richard Bishop when he approves the payroll, although variance investigation could be carried out by someone else. This person should be someone other than Cathy to restrict opportunity for payroll fraud.

Task 2

Tests of controls over hours worked

- Observation of staff clocking on and off

- Use of 'test data', ie dummy staff, to ensure that the clock operates efficiently

- Enquiry of management whether further controls operate to ensure individuals clock themselves off

- Review of clock reports for a week to ensure there are no obvious discrepancies (ie names appearing twice, unfeasible amount of hours)

- Review of clock reports for evidence of review and authorisation of hours worked by department heads

10

	Options
When an order is received Miss Dea, in sales, sends out a three-part pre-numbered despatch note to the inventory department	Weakness – no credit checks are made
The goods are sent to the despatch team, who send out the goods. They complete the despatch note, one copy is sent out with the goods, one copy is matched with the order and filed, the other is sent to the accounts department for invoicing	Strength – goods will not be invoiced unless sent out
Goods are invoiced by Mrs Soule, who also posts sales receipts to the ledger and manages credit control	Weakness – Mrs Soule deals with invoicing and credit receipts, there should be segregation of these duties

CHAPTER 5 Assessing risks

1   Industry, regulatory and other external factors, nature of the entity (including selection of accounting policies), objectives and strategies and business risks, performance measurement, internal control system

2   In order to be able to assess risks. This will then direct auditors as to what to test and how.

3   **Audit** risk is the risk that the auditors give an **inappropriate** opinion on the financial statements.

Control risk is the risk that the entity's internal control system will not prevent or detect and correct errors

Inherent risk is the risk that items will be misstated due to their **nature** or due to their **context**

Detection risk is the risk that errors will exist in financial statements and the auditors will not discover them

4

	Options
Auditors cannot affect inherent and control risk as inherent and control risks are the risks that errors will arise in the financial statements as a result of control problems or the nature of items in the financial statements of the entity. The auditors cannot control those factors.	True
If inherent and control risk are high, detection risk should be rendered low to come to an overall acceptable level of risk. In order for detection risk to be low, the auditors will have to carry out a low level of testing.	False – detection risk should be low, but to achieve that, auditors should carry out a high level of testing.

5

	Options
The control environment is weak and there is considerable pressure on management to improve results year-on-year.	Increase
Management has implemented improvements in controls as a result of weaknesses identified last year.	Reduce

6

	Options
Materiality is the concept of significance to users of the financial statements.	True
Performance materiality will usually be higher than materiality assessed for the financial statements as a whole.	False – it will be lower.

7

	Options
The company has diversified its operations during the year.	Increase
The company has discontinued operations in its riskiest operating area during the year.	Increase – although it might seem as though this would reduce risk, in this year, the company will have to meet accounting requirements relating to the changes, which increases audit risk.

CHAPTER 6   Audit planning

1   The audit **strategy** is the document that contains the general approach to the audit.

The audit **plan** is the document that contains the details of tests that will be carried out for each **account balance** or **class of transactions**.

Professional scepticism is an attitude of **awareness** that assumes neither honesty or dishonesty on the part of the directors but allows the auditor to observe and interpret relevant information as it becomes available to them during the audit.

2

	Options
At an audit team meeting the audit partner must emphasise the importance of professional scepticism.	True
An audit team must have a planning meeting only if the assessed risks are higher than anticipated.	False – they must always have one and discuss assessed risks.

3   Formulating audit procedures in an audit plan – this is a specific response: designing further audit procedures in specific risk areas.

4

	Options
Existence	Account balance
Valuation and allocation	Account balance
Cut-off	Classes of transaction

5   All sampling units should have an equal chance of being selected for testing. The other statements are all untrue.

6

	Options
Simran has been asked to select a sample of twelve sales invoices to trace from sales order to general ledger. There are sixteen folders of sales orders for the year, stored in the sales office.	Haphazard – where there is such a large population, Simran should select on a haphazard basis.
Julie has been asked to select a sample of five purchase ledger accounts to carry out a supplier statement reconciliation. There are 16 purchase ledger accounts.	Systematic – where there is a small population, ordered in a way that does not bias the sample (for example, alphabetically), systematic selection is suitable.
Ben is selecting a sample of inventory lines to perform a valuation test .The audit team have been instructed to use the computerised techniques available to them, one of which is a sample selection programme.	Random – if a random numbers programme is available it could be used as a suitable method of selecting a non-biased sample.

7

	Options
Increase in the auditor's assessment of the risk of material misstatement.	Increase
Increase in tolerable misstatement.	Decrease
Decision to stratify a large population.	Decrease

CHAPTER 7   Audit of inventory

1

	Options
Inventory is difficult to audit because it often consists of a large number of low value items which are collectively material.	True
Key assertions to test in relation to inventory are existence, completeness and valuation.	True

2   Auditors review inventory count instructions to assess whether the count is capable of producing an accurate figure for inventory existence.

3   Ensure that inventory count instructions are being followed and some substantive testing, such as observing damaged goods and obtaining cut-off details.

Auditors would evaluate the instructions at the planning stage, hence statement 1 is incorrect. Valuation is done after the count, so statement 3 is incorrect. Statement 4 is incorrect because the auditor never certifies that something is correct. He is observing the controls in operation at the count, not certifying its correctness.

4

	Options
It is important to record cut-off correctly so that assets are not double counted (receivables and inventory).	True
It is important to record cut-off correctly so that a liability is not omitted in respect of an asset (payables and inventory).	True
For the purposes of the financial statements, it does not matter if the company misstates cut-off between raw materials and work-in-progress.	False

5

	Options
Obtain evidence of the value of raw material.	Purchase invoice
Obtain evidence of the value of finished goods.	Both – finished goods will be tested for purchase price, cost of conversion, and also net realisable value (hence testing to after date sales invoices)

6   Net realisable value is tested with reference to after year-end **sales** so the value of items of inventory is compared with post year-end **sales invoices** to test that their value is equal to or **lower** than prices.

7   There appear to be several strong controls within the instructions (for example, Marie Edgehill, who is not usually connected with inventory, supervising, controls over the inventory records). However, there is one weakness connected with the actual counting. At present, the MEM instructions require one person to count and then the supervisors carry out random checks on the count.

It would be better practice to assign teams of two counters to each area – one to carry out the initial check and one to check every count that is made.

The random checks by the supervisors should highlight if counting has not been carried out carefully and recounts can be made if necessary. Despite this slight weakness in control, the count should still be capable of giving an accurate figure for existence.

8

	Options
Attending an inventory count.	Existence
Tracing counted items to final inventory sheets.	Completeness
Reviewing after year-end sales invoices.	Valuation

9 Sales cut-off appears to have been recorded properly. Purchases cut-off does not appear to have been recorded properly. Further tests should be carried out on deliveries received before the year-end.

10 Value correct   Purchase invoices

Lower than NRV   20X9 Sales price list

CHAPTER 8   Audit of other assets (and related items)

1 Auditors are concerned with **completeness, existence, rights and obligations and valuation**.

2 A key control is the non-current asset **register**, in which every asset should be recorded. Additionally, the company should ensure that additions and disposals are properly **authorised**.

3

	Options
Receivables circularisation	Rights and obligations – customers might agree that a debt is owed, but be unable to pay it.
Reviewing sales receipts after year-end	Both – looking at receipts after-date confirms valuation and that the company was owed that debt in the first place.

4

	Options
The receivables circularisation is sent out in the audit firm's name.	False – the client's name, although replies should be sent direct to the auditor.
Zero balances should not be included in the receivables circularisation.	False
The positive form of circularisation, where customers are asked to reply whether they agree the balance or not is the better form of receivables circularisation.	True

5 **Auditors usually rely 100% of controls over sales by carrying out only controls testing.** This is incorrect as sales is almost certainly a material balance, which must be subject to some detailed testing (which may be analytical procedures only or tests of detail or a combination). Auditors may choose not to test controls at all if they appear weak.

6

	Options
Bank letter requests are sent out by the auditor directly to the bank.	True – although the bank will only reply if the client have given them permission to.
Bank letter requests should be made at the year end date.	False. Requests should be made about a month in advance of the year-end to allow the bank time to process it.
Auditors will commonly test cash balances even if they are not material.	True – because cash is highly susceptible to fraud.

7 Tests to be carried out on non-current asset additions at MEM.

The auditors should carry out tests on the two material items. This sample, at nearly 100% of additions will be sufficient.

- Verify the cost and ownership of the machines to the purchase invoices.
- Physically inspect the machines to ensure that they exist.

8

Client: MEM	Prepared by:	Student
Accounting date: 31 December 20X8	Date:	9 April 20X9
	Reviewed by:	
	Date:	

Customer	Balance per ledger £	Reply received?	Balance agreed?	Reconciling items
Adams	27,354	Y	Y	N/A
Caterham	38,094	Y	N	Credit note £170 agreed
Dennings	46,299	N	–	
Eastern	323	Y	Y	
Fowlers	10,910	Y	Y	
Gunners	2,488	Y	Y	
Kellers	50,829	Y	N	Credit note £7,325 agreed – damaged goods
				Receipt £5,711 o/s
Mardons	36,592	Y	Y	
Murphys	4,588	Y	Y	
Petersham	982	Y	Y	
Timmins	3,601	N	–	
Walshes	12,933	Y	Y	

Further work required

(1) Need to follow-up replies from Dennings and Timmins. If no replies then received, should te by cash after-date.

(2) Need to verify receipt of £5,711 received after-date and assess whether receivables requires amendment. If amendment required, this balance should be extrapolated against receivable: balance and the result reviewed for materiality.

(3) Credit notes. These both appear genuine and should therefore be adjusted for. In addition, t auditors should review credit notes from just before the year-end to ensure that there are no others where cut-off appears to be incorrect and that should be adjusted.

(4) Inventory. In respect of the credit note for damaged goods, the auditors should see if they ca isolate whether those goods were included in the count and ensure that they have been valu appropriately if so.

9

```
Bank reconciliation for December 20X8
                                                              £
Balance per bank statement:                                "21,946
Cheques:                              XX0395√                 (395)
                                      XX0396√               (2,644)
                                      XX0397√               (4,766)
                                      XX0398√                 (477)
                                      XX0399√               (2,392)
                                      XX0400√                 (911)
                                      XX0401√                  (12)
                                      XX0402√               (5,783)
                                      XX0403√              (14,922)
Payments in:                          2044×                 12,944
                                      2045×                  3,928
                                      2046×                    322
Balance per cash book:                                       6,838

                            Audit key                           ^

                            ^ = Adds correctly
                            " = Agreed to bank letter
                            √ = Agreed to bank statements
                            after year-end date
                            × = Agreed to bank statements
                            after year-end date
```

CHAPTER 9   Audit of liabilities (and related items)

1   Auditors are concerned with completeness, existence and obligations.

2

	Options
They represent a better source of evidence than replies to a receivables circularisation as they are sent direct to the company.	False – this reduces their value as potentially they could be tampered with but they still represent a good source of third party evidence.
They are only used when the auditor is unable to do a payables circularisation.	False – an auditor would only carry out a payables circularisation in exceptional circumstances.
Testing supplier statements provides evidence that trade payables have not been understated.	True

3   Auditors should consider that payables might be **understated** and therefore not simply select large balances to test (although they must select **material** items). **Nil** balances should also be incorporated into the test.

4   **Accruals** are liabilities other than **trade creditors** that arise because the company has received a benefit it has not yet paid for.

Long-term liabilities are loans repayable at a date **more than** one year after the year-end.

5   Auditors are concerned with occurrence, accuracy and completeness.

6

Client: MEM				Prepared by:	Student
Accounting date: 31 December 20X8				Date:	10 April 20X9
				Reviewed by:	
				Date:	
Trade payables					
Payables	Balance per purchase ledger £	Balance per supplier statement £	Balance agreed	Comments	
Calais	156,498	156,498	Yes	€164,323 per statement @ year-end exchange rate = £156,498	
Denby	3,926	3,926	Yes		
John Johns	35,792	35,792	Yes		
Millars	20,692	20,692	Yes		
Wyndhams	2,967	N/A		No supplier statement available. Total agreed to invoice.	

Further work required

The Wyndhams balance has been agreed to the purchase invoice as there is no available statement for Wyndhams. We need to check why there is no statement available (they may not send them) and carry out a review of the usual invoice turnover and cost on the account to see if the balance appears reasonable.

7   **Purchases analysis**

20X7 shows purchases varying a little month-by-month, but basically being stable until December 20X7, when they jump considerably.

This may be because the company decided to stock up in December, but could also indicate that the cut-off at the year-end between December and January purchases was not measured accurately. The fact that purchases are low in January 20X8 could support either of these possibilities.

The auditor should have carried out additional cut-off tests in relation to December 20X7 in the previous year's audit and therefore the answer to this question should be given on the previous year's file. If cut-off was wrong and the accounts were adjusted, underlying records should also have been amended, so it is possible that the auditor is using an out-of-date schedule to review purchases.

20X8 shows a rising trend in purchases throughout the year. This could be as a result of increased productivity or an increase in costs. The auditor should make enquiries to see if either of these theories is borne out. An increase in productivity should be apparent in (hopefully) increased sales or alternatively, higher inventory levels. An increase in costs will be apparent from a review of purchase invoices.

No conclusion can be drawn at this stage as to whether purchases are fairly stated, as further work needs to be carried out to support the indications given by the analysis here.

8   Accruals at MEM

MEM is likely to have the following accruals:

Wages – if wages are paid in arrears	Should be a month's payroll, which can be agreed to the payroll.
PAYE	This should also agree to the payroll as it should be a month's deductions. It can also be verified to the after-date payment.
VAT – if the VAT returns are not coterminous with the year-end	This should be verifiable to the next VAT return.
Utilities	The company is likely to have paid standing charges for items such as gas, electricity and water in advance. These can be verified to the relevant invoices.

CHAPTER 10   Audit completion and reporting

1

	Options
Auditors must evaluate whether financial statements have been prepared in accordance with an applicable financial reporting framework.	True
Auditors must use analytical procedures when determining if the financial statements appear reasonable as a whole.	True

2   An entity is considered a **going concern** when it is likely to continue operating in the **foreseeable future**.

3

	Options
A responsibility to seek evidence of subsequent events and to ensure they are disclosed in financial statements.	Before audit report is signed
A responsibility to seek evidence that the financial statements are fairly stated when management brings subsequent events to their attention.	Both

4 The auditors need to consider the implications of the litigation on the financial statements on:

- Potential provision or disclosure required for the compensation

- Potential impact on going concern if the litigation gives ground for further claims

5 **Qualified opinion arising from disagreement about accounting treatment**

Basis for qualified opinion on financial statements

The company is in course of litigation with a former employee which could lead to the company needing to pay compensation of £X. In our opinion, the company is likely to have to make such a payment and provision of £X should have been made, reducing profit before tax and net assets by that amount.

In our opinion, except for the effects of to the matter described in the basis for qualified opinion paragraph, in our opinion the financial statements:

- Give a true and fair view of the state of the company's affairs as at 31 December 200X and of its profit [loss] for the year then ended.

- Have been properly prepared in accordance with United Kingdom Generally Accepted Accounting Practice, and

- Have been prepared in accordance with the Companies Act 2006

Opinion on other matter prescribed by the Companies Act 2006

In our opinion the information given in the directors' report for the financial year for which the financial statements are prepared is consistent with the financial statements.

Matters on which we are required to report by exception

[unchanged]

6

	Options
The auditors have discovered aggregate misstatements of £25,000 on the audit of Spring Cleaners Ltd. Materiality has been set at £100,000. The directors refuse to amend the financial statements.	Not modified
March Hare Ltd's largest customer has gone into liquidation. The directors do not want to write-off the debt owed by the customer which amounts to £25,000, which is material.	Modified

7   The audit firm's money laundering reporting officer

Test your learning – answers

INDEX

Notes

Notes

REVIEW FORM

How have you used this Text?
(Tick one box only)

☐ Home study

☐ On a course_____

☐ Other _____

Why did you decide to purchase this Text?
(Tick one box only)

☐ Have used BPP Texts in the past

☐ Recommendation by friend/colleague

☐ Recommendation by a college lecturer

☐ Saw advertising

☐ Other _____

During the past six months do you recall seeing/receiving either of the following?
(Tick as many boxes as are relevant)

☐ Our advertisement in Accounting Technician

☐ Our Publishing Catalogue

Which (if any) aspects of our advertising do you think are useful?
(Tick as many boxes as are relevant)

☐ Prices and publication dates of new editions

☐ Information on Text content

☐ Details of our free online offering

☐ None of the above

Your ratings, comments and suggestions would be appreciated on the following areas of this Text.

	Very useful	Useful	Not useful
Introductory section	☐	☐	☐
Quality of explanations	☐	☐	☐
How it works	☐	☐	☐
Chapter tasks	☐	☐	☐
Chapter overviews	☐	☐	☐
Test your learning	☐	☐	☐
Index	☐	☐	☐

	Excellent	Good	Adequate	Poor
Overall opinion of this Text	☐	☐	☐	☐

Do you intend to continue using BPP Products?   ☐ Yes   ☐ No

Please note any further comments and suggestions/errors on the reverse of this page. The author of this edition can be e-mailed at: suedexter@bpp.com

Please return to: Sue Dexter, Publishing Director, BPP Learning Media Ltd, FREEPOST, London, W12 8BR.

REVIEW FORM (continued)

TELL US WHAT YOU THINK

Please note any further comments and suggestions/errors below.